SMALL CRIMINALS AMONG US

SMALL CRIMINALS AMONG US

How to Recognize and Change Children's
Antisocial Behavior – Before They Explode

by
Gad Czudner, Ph.D.

New Horizon Press
Far Hills, New Jersey

Requests for permission should be addressed to:
New Horizon Press
P.O. Box 669
Far Hills, NJ 07931

Czudner, Gad
        Small Criminals Among Us: How to Recognize and Change Children's
        Antisocial Behavior – Before They Explode

Interior Design: Susan Sanderson

Library of Congress Catalog Card Number: 98-68327

ISBN: 0-88282-180-6

New Horizon Press

Manufactured in U.S.A.

2003   2002   2001   2000   1999 / 5   4   3   2   1

Contents

Author's Note

This book is based on my research, a thorough study of the available literature and over twenty years of counseling problem children, and child and adult criminals. Fictitious identities and names have been given to characters in this book in order to protect individual privacy, and some characters are composites. For the purposes of simplifying usage, the pronouns his and her are often used interchangeably.

Acknowledgements

Special thanks to Dr. Prem Gupta, the originator of the *Tough Talk* program at the Guelph Correctional Centre in Canada. Together we worked very hard in developing the cognitive moral approach for the treatment of criminality. I would also like to thank Frank Morton for his invaluable help in the early stages of the *Tough Talk* program. My efforts with children are to a large extent due to those initial endeavors.

I would also like to thank my wife, Mary Lou, for her many hours of proofreading and her creative and original ideas (plus the occasional argument as to which words read best). As well, her own integrity has always been a reminder to practice what I preach.

Also, I would like to thank Jo-Anne Shephard for her many hours of computing and for putting up with my temperament. I also greatly appreciate her assistance in organizing my ideas. Without her assistance and our regular "breaks," this book would never have been created.

I would also like to thank Dr. Samuel Yochelson and Dr. Stanton Samenow, who had the courage to show the world what a criminal is like, and Dr. William Glasser for providing me with the incentive to pursue the moral approach to the problem of criminality.

Finally, thanks to the Ministry of Solicitor General and Correctional Services and the Ministry of Education for allowing me to practice the *Tough Talk* program throughout numerous correctional facilities and schools in Ontario, Canada.

Introduction

In Richmond, California, a six-year-old boy who wanted to steal a tricycle sneaked into a neighbor's home and pulled one-month-old Ignacio Bermudez, Jr. out of his bassinet, placed him on the floor and kicked his head so hard that the baby's skull was fractured in four places, resulting in the likelihood that he may never walk.

In Liverpool, England, two ten-year-olds, Robert Thompson and Jon Venables, left the dead body of two-year-old James Bulger on the train tracks near their home. They had thrown twenty bricks at the small child's head, kicked him repeatedly, stripped, and possibly molested the boy.

In northeast Pennsylvania, nine-year-old Cameron Kocker shot seven-year-old Jessica Carr with a rifle and then hid it. They had had an argument over a video game.

In Englewood, a suburb of Chicago, a seven-year-old and his eight-year-old best friend became the two youngest murder suspects in the United States when they were accused of the murder and sexual assault of eleven-year-old Ryan Harris whose body was discovered in a vacant lot.

In Stockholm, Sweden, four-year-old Ken was strangled by two boys, ages five and seven, who pressed a stick to his throat, suffocating him after he was thrown on his back.

Though some children with serious behavior problems are rehabilitated toward normalcy by teachers, parents, and other authorities, such crimes as these demand that we take a serious new look at the risk factors of extremes of bad behavior in children today and seek ways to change them before such children explode.

When I started working with young and adult criminals some twenty years ago, I was still influenced by my psychological training which focused on the deterministic approach to psychological problems. This would suggest that every problem can be understood and solved if you recognize the cause. This may be true for medicine and pure science. However, I discovered when you deal with budding criminals or full-blown criminality, the problem is far too complex. After a few futile years of following that approach, I realized that all crime, whether perpetrated by a young child stealing from a grocery store, a teenager committing a break and enter, or children killing children, is motivated by self-interest.

I started searching for other ways of dealing with the problem of budding criminals and full-blown criminality. I came to recognize that the obsession with looking for causes of criminality doesn't help us to deal with children who are already expressing themselves in antisocial ways. While looking for causes may reveal correlations and give us leads for future application, this obsession does little to help us deal with the immense problem of child criminals today. Moreover, such a mind-set leads to excuses and rationalizations, which end up promoting criminality instead of eliminating criminal behavior.

Arguments about the origin of crime have been debated as long as the history of humanity. Some philosophers, like Thomas Hobbs, suggest that human nature is bad and morality is needed to control basic instincts. Others, like Jean Jacques Rousseau, argue the opposite, that human beings are born good and are corrupted by society. This is a chicken-and-egg approach which, in the treatment of budding criminals, leads us nowhere.

We must presume that each child is born with the potential for good or evil. He or she is born with a genetic disposition, meaning that a child's temperament is somewhat genetically influenced by his or her ancestors. With proper education, however, we can influence the direction a child will take. We are all familiar with the standard explanation that children who are neglected and abused are more likely to develop behavior problems or become criminals. Though this is true, it doesn't account for the children coming from such backgrounds who turn out well. And we mustn't forget there are some children with very positive upbringings who are difficult to socialize and for whom traditional methods of discipline seem ineffective.

The quest most relevant for our society today is to discover methods to prevent these problem children from turning into criminals. The question is not from where criminality comes, but how can we prevent or change the climate in which it grows. If we can identify warning signs in these defiant children early on, we can prevent criminality in young people before actual crimes occur.

In this book I will try to provide parents, teachers and others with a new method and some firm guidelines on how to tackle the problem of potentially delinquent children—the earlier the better. I have found neither punishment nor reward are effective methods for teaching morality.

Instead, I propose teaching pro-social behavior or moral values to children based not only on understanding but on feeling. Since emotions appear to be one of the sources that lead human beings to violence and criminality, they can also be used as tools to eliminate criminality or at least reduce it. To change problem behavior, the concept of arousing moral feeling—namely, empathy and guilt—is essential. Though many criminologists believe that criminals do not feel empathy, this has not been my finding. A small portion of the criminal population is incapable of feeling empathy. These individuals require highly specialized treatment programs. The rest, I suggest, are capable of experiencing strong feelings, especially for their loved ones. If these feelings are aroused, they will feel sufficient guilt to provide strong motivation for change. Empathy, which is innate in human beings, is part of our genetic makeup as social beings. It is a prerequisite for guilt.

I would like to help parents, educators and professionals to view the problem somewhat differently and attempt my method of dealing with such difficult children. Many teachers and parents with whom I have been in contact over the last twenty years and who were willing to try my method write their appreciation. I do not pretend to have a panacea to crime. I only want to follow some radical new ideas that I first pointed out in my paper, "Changing the Criminal." They suggest, as do the breakthrough theories in William Glasser's *Reality Therapy*, that a person is not bad because he is sick, rather the opposite—he is sick because he is bad.

In the first four chapters of this book, I will try to show parents that criminality can be prevented if the problem is properly detected in the young. I realize that many parents may be appalled by my suggestion that their toddlers could turn into criminals. Yet, the problem of childhood crime is sufficiently serious that if they ignore it or deny it, much sorrow could follow.

I will also argue with professionals who emphasize that morality is based on understanding moral values and try to ignore the *feeling* aspect of morality. Moral intelligence is based on understanding and feeling. Only harmony between the two can prevent the development of criminality. Such harmony will also help us to become better human beings, even though we may never end up in jail.

There are many books about love, and I do not pass myself off as an expert on this emotion. I do believe, however, that some of the mistakes made in the name of love can be corrected by using the methods described in this book.

In a later chapter of this book, I will talk about the many children who may not end up in jail, but are not nice children. By the same token, if we ignore some of the warning signs I describe in these willful children, we may contribute to the development of a very dangerous child. It is very possible that children who are addicted to power will commit violent acts either in the context of gang activities or as individuals.

In another chapter, I discuss my method to change defiant children. It can be applied to all age groups. With a few minor changes, it can be applied to adults as well.

The significance of empathy and guilt is also emphasized. Parents will see how empathy is an important aspect of love and needs to be taught to young children so that they are unlikely to develop into criminals. Though guilt is generally viewed as a negative emotion in traditional psychological literature, I use it as a positive aspect of human character and submit that guilt focused on others is a guide for moral action.

Finally, I would like to suggest that psychological theories encouraging morbid introspection, preoccupied self-awareness, self-love, self-esteem and self-respect often achieve the opposite results from what they are seeking. Only by the constant movement from self to others can one become more human. That is the true meaning of love and spirituality. Only by loving others can you love yourself.

Hence, the most important thing in raising children is to constantly look for activities that encourage giving rather than taking and sharing rather than keeping for oneself.

The Bible says, "Love thy neighbor as thyself." I would suggest, "Love thy neighbor without focusing on self." Albert Einstein said, "Man's ultimate goal is liberation from the self." This is the ultimate goal of morality and humanity!

In spite of obstacles inherent in our economic and social structure, the survival of the one and the survival of the many should not be in conflict.

I realize that many of the ideas I contribute in this book are somewhat controversial, and I hope that they will spark debate. I believe that the truth about children whose warning signs show they may become criminals as I have learned it in over two decades of treating young criminals needs to be said. Progress does not come from conformity!

Juvenile crime is rising both in number and seriousness. If we do not find new ways of habilitating and rehabilitating the small criminals among us, what is the alternative?

1

A Day in the Lives of Two Budding Criminals (Ages Four and Seven)

Diane, age four, was the daughter of two working parents; her mother was a nurse and her father a construction worker. The parents were both hard working people who were very concerned about raising good children. Diane had an older sister, Emily, who was seven. Emily was a good girl, responsible, helpful, very sociable, a good student and a source of pride for both parents.

Diane was a disaster. She was a colicky baby, constantly screaming from the day she was born. She slept very little, and as soon as she could talk, always insisted that she wanted to be in her parents' bed. Though the exasperated parents tried, they always ended up giving into Diane's threats and tantrums.

Seldom did the parents leave her with a baby-sitter for an evening because no sitter could handle her. One confided to Diane's father that she had confined Diane to her bed because she was afraid the girl would either destroy the furniture or hurt herself.

At the age of four, Diane was introduced to nursery school. In the morning, both girls were awakened at seven o'clock to prepare for breakfast and school. Diane never got up peacefully—she was angry from the moment she woke up, screaming and demanding; breakfast was usually a fight between Diane and her sister, Emily. Yet, Emily was patient with Diane.

On one Tuesday morning, Diane threw pancakes at her sister because she claimed Emily said something Diane did not like, which Emily, of course, denied. Past experience suggested that Diane usually lied; Emily rarely lied.

Both girls had lived in the same home since birth and the parents tried very hard to show no favoritism; therefore, it is difficult to explain how the environment caused one girl to be so different from the other.

When the struggle over breakfast ended, Diane was finally dressed and her mother took her to nursery school while Emily took the bus. Conflicts were avoided for a short while. However, when Diane arrived at school, more problems started.

Mrs. Snow, the nursery school teacher, was an experienced teacher who tried her best to accommodate Diane but had little success. Within the first half-hour of school, Diane pulled a chair out from under Sari, a classmate, hurting Sari when she fell down—Diane thought it was funny. When she was revealed as the culprit, Diane denied it and said the fall was an accident.

Barely an hour later when the children in the class were given the task of coloring for a short period, Diane began the task but then quickly tired of it. She began to tear pages out of the coloring book. She seemed to take great delight in mischievous activity. Mrs. Snow was worried that Diane would be a bad influence on the other children but hesitated to isolate her. In order to cope with her bad behavior, the teacher put Diane in the front row. One would be really amazed how, from there, she could manage to pick a fight with girls at the back of the room, but Diane was creative. She wadded up balls of paper and threw them whenever the teacher's eyes were turned away from her.

At ten o'clock, during snack time, snacks began disappearing from other girls. Diane even threw another child's sandwich on the floor. Again, Diane took great delight in seeing the misfortune of the other girls.

Around eleven o'clock, when the teacher was at the black-board, a boy started to cry very loudly. Diane had bit him. At that point, the teacher tried to engage Diane in a serious discussion about how unfair it was to bite another child. Diane claimed that it was retaliation for the boy's pulling on her dress.

Finally, it was time for the children to leave. The teacher felt she'd been in a war zone. Diane was ready to face her mother who had arrived to take her home. As soon as Diane saw her mother, she started screaming again. Diane told her mother that several girls in the nursery school were not nice to her and she did not want to go there anymore. The mother managed to coax the child out the door with the promise of treats.

The trip home was very unpleasant as Diane was screaming the entire time. She truly saw herself as the victim of the class and the teacher, and she protested loud and clear that she would not go back to nursery school.

During the afternoon when the mother returned to work, Diane was left with a baby-sitter. This was the fourth baby-sitter that had been hired to care for Diane over the past two years. This last one was an older woman with grown children who took the job believing that she could handle Diane. The parents had to pay extra money.

Despite the baby-sitter's belief in her ability to control the girl, Diane decided to sneak out of the house around two o'clock when the baby-sitter was in the bathroom. The woman panicked and immediately called the police and Diane's mother. Where was the child? When police and the hysterical mother arrived, a search of the neighborhood began. The police found Diane in a nearby home. She was wrestling with a four-year-old neighbor child, and the mother of the boy was having obvious difficulty controlling the two of them. The neighbor was embarrassed about the whole incident but insisted that Diane had told her she had permission to go to their home to play with her son. Diane's mother reprimanded her daughter, "You'll have to spend the remainder of the day and evening in your own room, and I'm taking the TV set out."

The punishment did not last very long because Diane attempted to break a window in her room. Fearing Diane might harm herself, her mother gave in, brought the TV set back and let Diane watch her favorite television programs.

When Diane's father came home from work around six o'clock, he went in to see her. Diane protested violently to him that everyone had treated her badly that day. She put her cute little face up to her dad and he completely melted. Of course, he comforted her, saying that there would be better days, and wondered why Diane should be so badly treated.

At the dinner table, Diane insisted that she did not want the spaghetti her mother made for dinner and only wanted ice cream. She also complained that Emily ate ice cream yesterday and did not have to eat her dinner (another lie). Since the parents had already been through quite a bit that day, they gave in and let Diane have all the ice cream she wanted before going to bed. It was another instance of her very intelligent manipulation of her parents, and her ability to control was getting more and more predominant.

Both getting up in the morning and going to bed were always disasters for Diane. In the evenings, she would scream so loudly that her parents would give up, letting her go to bed much later than her older sister—sometimes ten or eleven o'clock at night. When the parents consulted a psychologist, not long before I saw them, he had advised them not to give in. "Diane should go to bed at seven o'clock," he insisted. At that point, however, Diane had gained a lot of power—she agreed to obey on the condition that she would have a television in her room and her favorite toys. Even though she was in her room, she did not have to go to bed—she won again.

Without intervention, what kind of woman would Diane grow up to be? That scenario can give you a good idea—she will probably be cruel, dishonest, and destructive. Her needs for power and control will only grow, and her lack of empathy will provide fertile soil for the budding criminal to flourish.

At four, Diane was a terror, but other types of defiant children show budding criminal traits early in more subtle ways: meet Bruce.

Bruce was the seven-year-old only son of middle-aged parents who were married late in life and were very happy to have a child. He was a good boy when he was a baby, but the trouble started around the age of five when Bruce, an intelligent child, was sent early to first grade.

His parents had spoiled Bruce and when he started school, he found it very difficult to tolerate attention being given to other students—he wanted to be the teacher's pet, as he had always had his parents' undivided attention. Bruce felt that he was special and unique, and he let you know that very quickly. Unlike Diane, getting up in the morning was never a problem for Bruce. Breakfast was always a very special occasion. He always got what he wanted to eat, and unfortunately, he was growing obese because of the amount of food he consumed. Since he loved stacks of pancakes, he seldom ate anything else.

Bruce had never attended nursery school because his parents thought he was too precious. Now each morning, as he went off to first grade, Bruce would alternate between temper tantrums and fits of depression. On one Monday, he told his teacher that he was feeling very, very unhappy.

John Abbott, the teacher, was worried and decided to ask Bruce's parents to make an appointment with a local doctor. Horrified, the parents quickly complied. The doctor said there seemed to be no organic cause for the depression. The school psychologist, who was also consulted, suggested that the home be investigated as to the cause of Bruce's depression. When problems arise in school, professionals often look for trouble at home and tend to blame the problem on the parents. Bruce was a very manipulative child and knew quite well what he was doing.

On Tuesday morning, the acting out of his depression was so severe that it distracted the rest of the class and disrupted the program the teacher was trying to teach. The excitement spurred Bruce on. Since neither the doctor nor the school psychologist had found reasons, John Abbott was still at a loss as to why Bruce was depressed. He sent Bruce to the principal, Mr. Conway, who asked Bruce why he was so unhappy. Bruce said, "I don't like the teacher. I want to have another one right away." This time he wanted a "female" teacher.

Bruce's only friend, Mark, had a female teacher and, during recess, Mark always praised the female teacher for giving the class whatever they wanted. Bruce liked what he heard and decided that was for him. He immediately put his plan to change teachers into effect. Bruce and Mark were both loners who seldom played with other children but seemed to get along with each other, because Mark always let Bruce have his way.

Another disturbing trait that Bruce had begun to exhibit was that, despite his intelligence, Bruce neglected to do the work in class and was caught cheating several times on both tests and home-work. One of the projects Mr. Abbott had assigned required the class to be divided into several groups. The children were supposed to build a church steeple out of small blocks. Bruce only put a cou-ple of blocks together and spent the rest of the time apart from the others, pretending to be busy. When the project was complete, he was the first to declare loudly that he was the designer and builder of the structure. Only a keen observer would realize that he was try-ing to take credit for something he did not do.

At lunch break, all the children brought sandwiches. The night before, Bruce had insisted his mother get Kentucky Fried Chicken. While all the other kids ate sandwiches, he ate five pieces of chicken. When his friend Mark asked him for a piece, Bruce laughed at him, saying, "This is mine!"

Just before the end of the day, Mr. Abbott noticed he was missing a pair of scissors from his desk. He asked the class who had taken the scissors, but they all denied any knowledge. On the way home from school that day on the school bus, Bruce sat in the back with his friend Mark. Suddenly, there was a lot of commotion at the back of the bus. A small young girl was crying as Bruce threatened her with the scissors and attempted to cut off her necklace and take it home. When the bus driver tried to stop the commotion, Bruce immediately suggested that the girl had offered to give him the neck-lace in exchange for the pair of scissors he was wielding, which he claimed to have found at the back of the school yard. The girl denied Bruce's story, and it seemed suspicious to the bus driver. So, when he arrived at Bruce's bus stop, the driver told Bruce's parents about the necklace and the scissors. When Bruce's parents asked the boy what had happened, he replied, "I wasn't going to cut her. I found the scissors and the girl offered me the necklace, because she wanted the scissors." Of course the girl had denied the story, but since the parents did not talk to her, they naturally believed Bruce.

At supper time when Bruce demanded a hamburger, fries, and a milkshake from a fast food restaurant, his father went out to get them. Although Bruce ate an enormous amount, he was not curtailed because his parents always felt Bruce should have what he wanted. After all, they did not want to frustrate his needs and believed their leniency would give their son the kind of love they never had.

After dinner, Bruce insisted that he be allowed to watch an extremely violent movie, to which his parents acceded, against their better judgment. Like Diane, going to bed was a problem for Bruce. In fact, this night was no different than any other night. He insisted on sleeping in his parents' bed, and, once again, his parents did not object.

What kind of a man will Bruce grow up to be? That scenario can give you a good idea—he probably will be manipulative, dishonest, cruel, and somewhat grandiose. Since he has been obsessed, even at his young age, with food, it will most likely only be a question of time until he progresses to other substances, such as cigarettes, drugs, and alcohol. Will his parents be able to stop him? Probably not.

Despite the awful portraits I have drawn of these two problem children, I believe the bad traits and behaviors of children like Bruce and Diane can be changed and replaced with positive traits and behavior. I am not sure that all of them can be replaced, but even if we replace some, we are moving in the right direction. How to do this will be discussed in detail in later chapters.

2

Prevention

The earlier we identify a child with a potential for criminality, the better chance there is of successfully preventing criminality from developing. The best theory of prevention I have found is based on two ideas: 1) diagnosis and 2) correction.

To make an accurate diagnosis, we must first rule out medical problems. A neurologist or pediatrician should examine the child before he is referred to a psychologist. This doesn't mean that if a neurological or medical problem is diagnosed, it is an excuse for antisocial, criminal behavior.

However, when there is a diagnosis of Attention Deficit Disorder (ADD) or dyslexia involved, the prevention of criminality will require additional effort. Obviously, if a child is schizophrenic or autistic, a different approach to preventing the development of more serious antisocial behavior is required.

A diagnosis has two potential components: a problem and a deficit. A problem centers on the choices the child makes and/or the environmental conditions influencing the child and can be treated by a psychologist. A deficit usually indicates a medical condition treatable by a medical doctor.

As a psychologist, I mainly focus on problems. Nevertheless, I will keep emphasizing that a deficit is not an excuse for the development of criminality. Traditional thinking on making a diagnosis of a budding criminal is still very deterministic. That is, it is influenced by the medical, biological, scientific or sociological method that suggests every cause has an effect. This approach tends to ignore what I consider a very important component, the child's ability to make free choices, even at the age of three or four.

When I am trying to diagnose potential criminality, I look for the most serious warning signs and teach the adults dealing with the child how to rate the child from zero to ten in terms of each risk trait. Zero is given when the child shows no sign of the trait, while ten indicates the child exhibits the trait all the time. The traits are: self-centeredness, lying, low frustration tolerance, lack of empathy, lack of discipline, stealing, and power and control. With seven traits to rate, the highest possible score is seventy.

In one case, the parents of Matthew, a five-year-old boy, brought him to my clinic. At our first meeting, he was generally oppositional, having strong reactions to the word "no" in almost every situation. Next, I learned Matthew was selective in his toilet habits. He consistently messed his pants at home, but never while at school. Obviously, he was trying to tell us something.

In a sense, the boy was behaving badly almost to spite his parents. Interestingly enough, the parents were medical and social workers, as well as psychologists. With their special knowledge and expertise, the parents found it especially upsetting that the boy was soiling his pants.

I first asked the parents to rate Matthew in terms of the warning signs on the scale of zero to ten. Using the variable of lying, for example, they were to give him a ten if he lied all the time, a five if he lied occasionally, and a one or two if he hardly every lied.

High scores by Matthew on each of the variables would result in an overall high score of between sixty and seventy. Moderate scores on each would create an overall score of thirty-five, and so on. In addition, I asked the parents to pay close attention to a high score on any particular variable. Even if Matthew scored less than thirty overall, but had one or two individual high scores, we would see that as a bad sign.

As it turned out, Matthew's overall score was only thirty, which is not too serious. However, he scored eight on low frustration tolerance—which explains his reaction to the word "no"—and eight on power and control. He scored a three or four on each of the remaining traits.

I suggested to the parents that we first try to stop the toilet problem and afterward deal with the other signs of Matthew's defiant behavior. To eliminate the problem of Matthew's soiling of his pants, I felt that it would be best to have Matthew face the consequences of his actions.

I told the parents that if he did it again (they would know immediately because he usually protested or screamed when it happened), they should let him walk around with his dirty pants for some time. If this approach failed to cure the problem, they should let Matthew wash his own pants. If that failed, they should put Matthew back into diapers and treat him like a baby because he was behaving like one. I also asked the parents to explain to Matthew that this was what would happen as long as his behavior persisted.

One week later, I received a telephone call from Matthew's father telling me that Matthew had not had an accident in over a week. The father said they skipped the initial procedures and simply told Matthew that if he soiled his pants again, they would put a diaper on him. The diaper threat did the trick! Matthew's parents were very excited that they did not have to resort to further methods.

Matthew's attempt to get control over his parents was highly selective and expressed by his toilet habits. If we had used the traditional treatment approach, we would have assumed that his toilet habits were connected to insecurity, attempts to gain attention, lack of love, etc. This wasn't true. Matthew simply made a choice to get control, which is a significant warning sign in the development of criminality. Next, we dealt with the other warning signs where Matthew scored highly.

To ensure that a diagnosis is accurate, parents need to be taught to understand the warning signs of potential criminality. Then, most will not have difficulty rating their child's behavior. However, some parents are in denial and do not want to admit that their child is a potential antisocial, budding criminal.

If I ascertain this is the case, I recommend that someone more objective do the rating. Also, to ensure validity and reliability in the rating, I like to have two independent people do the rating without discussing it with each other, so I often enlist a teacher, relative, or a close family friend. Obviously, many parents see their child as a projection of themselves and are often too embarrassed to admit a fault in their offspring. This type of parent has difficulty using my method and usually prefers a traditional approach in treatment.

During a recent four-hour airplane flight, I had the opportunity to watch a five-year-old girl's behavior. She was very cute and seemed intelligent. She was sitting in the first row next to a window and had a book on her lap but was looking out at the sky. The flight crew began to show a movie. The girl could not see the movie from the first row, and the bright sunlight from her window made it impossible for others to watch it.

The flight attendant asked the girl to pull down the shade on the window. She obliged for five minutes and then opened the shade again. Her teenage sister was sitting next to her and asked her to pull the shade down. The girl did so again for another two minutes but then put the window shade up again, protesting that she was looking at pictures in her book and that the reading light wasn't strong enough for her. I observed the girl closely, noticing that she was really not too interested in her book, but was only interested in pulling the shade up, probably as an act of defiance.

For the next fifteen minutes a struggle ensued between the older sister and the younger one. The younger one put the shade up, and the older one pulled it down. Eventually, the young girl won the battle, and, for the remainder of the movie it was very difficult for the one hundred or so other passengers to see it clearly. The little girl maintained total control of the aircraft.

I also noticed that she was bad-mouthing her sister throughout the struggle.

If we were to rate the child on the seven warning signs, the young girl would score ten on power and control, and probably ten on low frustration tolerance. I believe that if I had really been testing her, she would have scored very close to seventy, with tens on most of the warning signs.

Anti-criminal aptitudes or skills may develop in young children from a very early age, perhaps as early as a year old. These aptitudes may be defined in terms of three major concepts:

1) **social intelligence**
2) **emotional intelligence**
3) **moral intelligence.**

Research in this field indicates that no one systematically separates the three concepts. They are similar but still differ in many ways.

Social intelligence implies manners, customs or cultural habits and may be defined in the way children and adults interact with one another. Saying "please," "thank you," and "I beg your pardon" are expressions showing social intelligence. Sitting appropriately at a dinner table without one's elbows on it and using a fork and knife properly are other examples.

Any behavior suggesting a child's respect of peers, adults, and parents is, to a large extent, social intelligence. My own daughter was always quiet, polite, charming, and helpful in many ways from an early age. This has carried through to her adult years, and she is still very charming and well liked by others.

Low social intelligence can be seen in a child who causes scenes in public places. Usually the scene is motivated by an attempt to gain control and get what the child wants. Such a child might use profanity when told to do something or get in trouble from the first day at school. Parents probably need to look for new baby-sitters constantly to deal with the child. Such children have no respect for others and are typically referred to as brats.

I noted high social intelligence in another child I observed on another airline flight. She was about two years old and held her toy which she called "George" as she walked in the aisle with her mother. I asked her if I could play with George for a few minutes. The child hesitated a moment, looked at me and looked at her mother, who said nothing. The young girl decided to let me have George, even though she was apprehensive as to whether she would get him back. When I returned George after a short minute, she smiled and said, "Thank you." I believe this young child showed both social and likely moral intelligence because she was willing to share and exhibited polite manners.

Emotional intelligence is defined quite extensively by Dr. Daniel Goleman in his book, *Emotional Intelligence*. He lists five areas of emotional intelligence:
1) knowing one's emotions (meaning self-awareness and ability to recognize feeling)
2) managing the feelings or emotions
3) using feelings to motivate one's behavior
4) recognizing feelings in others
5) handling relationships

Low emotional intelligence is displayed by a child who does not express feelings and is withdrawn. He reacts to every situation with apparent indifference. Such a child could be potentially depressed and, at times, could become violent because his feelings are suppressed.

A child with high emotional intelligence is in touch with his feelings and is able to freely express sorrow, joy, excitement, and happiness in a spontaneous, loving way. Such behavior seems natural. Usually this child is close to a mother who is empathetic and loving and who provides the child with sufficient emotional room to express feelings freely and spontaneously. Such a parent is also able to discriminate between feelings of anger when it is used to manipulate and get control and anger when it is caused by frustration or pain.

Moral intelligence is defined in terms of the child's ability to show consideration for others, to have respect, and mostly to show sympathy and empathy. As the child advances in age, he or she may reach altruism, the peak of emotional intelligence.

A highly moral child is usually more than willing to share. If she has siblings, she will be protective of them rather than jealous, particularly if she is older. A child who shows low moral intelligence seldom, if ever, shows empathy. She never shares; she screams at any annoying situation; and she is extremely noisy if she does not get her own way. It is easy to define such low moral intelligence by applying the seven warning signs of budding criminal behavior. Chances are, such a child will score between sixty and seventy when rated.

The best prevention against children developing into criminals is instilling moral values at an early age. Traditional developmental psychologists generally view moral development in terms of cognitive abstract abilities. Lawrence Kohlberg's book, *Stage and Sequences*, and Jean Piaget's book, *The Moral Judgment of the Child*, suggest that a child usually moves from an extremely egocentric stage to universal morality. Obviously, a child's concept of morality is very egocentric and can be expressed as, *What's good for me is good for everyone else.* In this theory, when a two-year-old tells his mother, "I love you," he evaluates love in terms of what his mother can do for him.

Dr. Kohlberg suggests that children develop from a pre-conventional type of morality (level one) to conventional morality (level two). When they become adults, they may develop post-conventional morality. For most children under the age of nine and some adolescents (especially criminal adolescents), the idea of morality is based on authority rather than understanding. For example, if you ask such a child, "Why is it wrong to steal from a store?" He will tell you, "It's against the law," rather than "It will hurt the store owner."

Even a young criminal knows that crime is wrong, but he does not know why. This level two (conventional morality) is where most adolescents and many adults stay. Many adults believe there are rights and wrongs because society says so.

Level three (post-conventional morality) is only reached by very few people—a minority of adults and very few children. It is based on understanding the universal principal of morality, meaning, when you steal you violate someone's rights. I would like to add here that one of my main criticisms of this method is that it ignores the emotional aspect of morality which I call moral feeling. It is the instilling of moral feeling which I believe is most important. This is advanced by the feminist movement and by Dr. Carol Gilligan.

Lawrence Kohlberg developed his theory by presenting moral dilemmas to children. It was clear from the way the children related to these dilemmas that their thinking was based on right and wrong concepts as the basis for moral thinking. Kohlberg asked an eleven-year-old boy to assess a situation where a man was faced with his wife dying unless he stole certain drugs to save her life, as he had no money to pay for the medication. The boy suggested that it was all right to steal in this case in order to save a human life. The boy felt his reasoning was logical, since he believed saving a life was more important than theft.

When Amy, an eleven-year-old girl, was asked the same question posed by Kohlberg, she said there might be another way besides stealing. She said perhaps the man could borrow money to buy the drugs to save his wife. She remarked that if the man did steal to save his wife's life, he would end up in jail and be of no use to her.

Carol Gilligan, author of *In a Different Voice*, suggested that the boy's solution to the dilemma was analyzed like a mathematical problem while the girl's solution was viewed in terms of relationships. Amy looked at the crime as affecting the relationship. The boy suggested that, in some cases, crime is justified. He was not concerned about the effect of the crime on the man's wife and family.

I suggested in my own paper, "Changing the Criminal," that the difficulty in teaching morality using Lawrence Kohlberg's method is that the basis for rational understanding of morality is

not a sufficient deterrent to crime. On the other hand, if we emphasize the effect of the crime on the victim or the criminal's own family, it may serve as a deterrent, especially if empathy can be developed and sustained throughout life.

Twenty years of experience with both young and adult criminals demonstrates to me that those who change their criminal
behavior do so in most part because they start feeling the pain and
hurt of the people they love and see themselves as directly responsible for that pain. That phenomenon works in children and adults
alike. Later in this book, I discuss how adolescents and juvenile
offenders develop effective strategies to block their innate capacity
for empathy. An infant or toddler does not yet possess such strategies, which is why it is relatively easy to effectively teach empathy to
very small children.

There are many observations to show that empathy is a natural spontaneous phenomenon in babies. Nancy Eisenberg quotes
Ross Thompson: "At fourteen months, Susan noticed a crying six-
month-old baby. She watched for a while and then tears filled her
eyes and she began to cry."

In another situation, Michael, at fifteen months, was fighting with his friend Paul over a toy and Paul started to cry. Michael
appeared disturbed and let go of the toy, but Paul still cried. Michael
pushed Paul and then brought his teddy bear to him. Yet his friend
continued crying. Michael then decided to fetch Paul's security blanket from another room. This worked—Paul stopped crying.

This is a good example. If Michael were a potential criminal,
he would likely have been indifferent to Paul, possibly even kicking
him after taking his toy. In that case, I strongly suggest that the consequences of his actions should be severe enough that Michael
would realize he cannot kick Paul and take his toy. Also, the teaching of empathy could be reinforced by showing Michael how much
his mother, father or anyone else Michael likes is disturbed by his
poor uncaring attitude toward his friends.

I would like to emphasize that the teaching of empathy,
respect and consideration for others can be done by anyone who
knows the techniques and understands the value of the concepts.

In my own practice, I continuously advise parents to show their own anguish when a child misbehaves, so that the problem child can connect one event of hurting to the pain of the parents.

If a child is hurting a stranger, he may have trouble feeling the stranger's pain. However, if the child has a strong relationship with an adult, he can be taught to experience the pain his actions have on that adult.

Empathy should be taught consistently to replace selfish and hurtful behavior the child shows towards peers, adults, animals or even himself. Of course, the child who already displays the warning signs of developing criminality will be harder to teach, but positive results almost guarantee that criminality will not develop further.

Michael Schulman and Eva Mekler in their excellent book, *Bringing Up a Moral Child*, suggest that moral training should start from the day the child is born. They also emphasize that only a loving mother or father is able to teach moral values. They suggest that if a child of ten months is too rough with a pet or a brother or sister, the parent should take the child's hand and say, "Be nice, be gentle." At that age, children learn by imitation.

As well, at the age of ten months or so, a parent can begin to teach the child to share. Sharing should not be negotiable and should be done consistently. The message the parent gives should be, *if the child doesn't share, the child doesn't get!*

My own children loved playing with Legos. I always encouraged them to try to build things together and praised them if they were successful. If you have an only child, invite a neighbor's child or let the child share with an adult for practice. Let the adult get on the floor and play at the child's level. The child will appreciate the game, and the experiences will remain with him for the rest of his life.

I find adults speak with nostalgia about parents who were able to play with them at their level—building castles, riding a bicycle, going fishing, or whatever. Children say the same thing. They will never build a relationship with an adult who attempts to control and discipline them without love. In fact, if you are loving enough with a child and provide enough opportunity for him to explore his environment and play different games with him, discipline becomes much easier.

If, as I believe, empathy is the most important aspect of moral intelligence, then the way we raise boys and girls contributes to disharmony between the sexes as well as to violence, especially among boys. I like to see boys being allowed to play with dolls and girls being allowed to play with cars. There should not be such a clear difference between the way we raise boys and girls.

Carol Gilligan's concept of morality based on building relationships makes much more sense to me than putting all the emphasis on the understanding of moral principles. I have had leaders in my therapy groups in jail who show clear understanding of moral principles, yet they remain very dangerous and commit further outrageous crimes when released from custody. Why? They never really felt the pain and hurt of the victim or the victim's family that resulted from their actions.

Sometimes, babies and toddlers cry, argue or use other disrespectful behavior as a means to get their own way. I believe most mothers can distinguish between a cry based on genuine need, such as hunger pain and real discomfort, and a cry designed to get control and manipulate. If a parent allows a baby who cries to gain control and achieve her goal, the baby will quickly learn the benefits of crying, and by the time the baby is two years of age, she will have control of the house. If this happens with a potentially criminal child, that control and power can be dangerous, eventually leading to serious criminality. Even if she does not become a criminal, the parent is raising a self-centered baby, and it will be very difficult to take that child to a shopping mall, restaurant, or on a trip without experiencing a scene.

How does one teach respect? For instance: whenever the child uses profane language, punish the child for it. The punishment should be short and timely. If a child swears at his mother, the mother should take his favorite toy away immediately and tell him that he will only get the toy back if he apologizes and approaches her with respect. If he doesn't know how to do this, the mother must show him.

The second stage of teaching is to replace one behavior with another. I find this technique an effective one with young children. If a child breaks a friend's toy, she must replace it with one of her toys of equal value. If she does not, use punishment again (perhaps by taking several of her toys away). Since the potential criminal is extremely hedonistic and pleasure-seeking, the most effective punishment with her is to remove something that she likes or to introduce something she likes and then take it away.

Recently, I interviewed a mother in my clinic who suggested her five-year-old son consistently treated his sister and his stepfather with disrespect. Since he liked his mother, he did not treat her disrespectfully. I invited the stepfather, sister and the boy to the clinic, and we practiced respectful behavior.

As he and I related well to each other, he started practicing respectful behavior in order to please me. On one occasion I asked him to say something to his stepfather politely, "Can we go for ice cream today, please?" If he did not say "please," I showed disapproval and I threatened that I would not see him again. I always spent the first half-hour playing games with him, and he was terrified of losing this opportunity. The more such a child practices respectful behavior, the more likely it will become a habit.

Generally, I find that parents emphasize punishment rather than replacing negative behavior with positive behavior. However, one punishment that is effective with youngsters is "time out," in which the child is placed in a room by himself. Another way to punish a child is to take away some object or privilege that the child enjoys. The more you are able to teach pro-social behavior as a substitute for antisocial behavior very early in childhood, the less likely you will have to use punishment later on.

As a consultant for a school board, I have frequently dealt with toddlers who disrupt their classes. Experienced teachers usually find a good way to deal with these children. However, the inexperienced teacher is sometimes very frustrated with this type of child and asks that the child be relocated to another class or, in some instances, the teacher considers quitting teaching altogether.

Not long ago, I was called into school to consult with the staff about Susie, who was four years old and came from a single-parent home. There was some evidence that the family was dysfunctional. The mother had been abused by her husband and spent a few months in a women's shelter. Susie was placed with the Children's Aid Society during that time. As soon as Susie joined nursery school, trouble started. She would not sit in a chair for more than five minutes. Children were given tasks like building with blocks, coloring, and learning the alphabet. Susie refused to listen to the instructions or to participate in the activities. She consistently instigated fights with boys in the classroom.

The teacher referred Susie for intelligence testing. At such a young age this testing is not too reliable. However, the psychologist who administered the test concluded that Susie was functioning slightly below average intelligence. Most traditional psychological literature suggests that when dealing with children who have below average intelligence, behavior modification is the most effective method of changing undesirable behavior.

Behavior modification, which can be effective at certain times, is based on rewarding good behavior and punishing bad behavior. However, when the nursery school teacher approached me for advice, I suggested that we attempt to deal with Susie using the cognitive moral method, emphasizing the increase of moral intelligence. Surprisingly (or maybe not surprisingly), Susie was a very affectionate little girl. Perhaps the fact that she received inconsistent love at home created a need for Susie to desperately look for love. I felt that need could be utilized by the teacher to form a relationship with Susie. We could then start applying my method, using some of the techniques I've already described.

My rationale was that, even though some undesirable behavior could be eliminated by using the traditional methods, the little girl would not really change to become a better person if she did not understand and feel the impact her negative behavior was having on her teacher and classmates.

I asked the teacher if I could sit in the class and observe Susie. During the first morning's class, the children were separated into small groups and were asked to draw a picture, with each child in the group using a different color to complete the picture. Susie appeared almost incapable of working in cooperation with the other children.

I suggested that I take Susie and one other child, and the three of us would work on the project together while the teacher dealt with the rest of the class. Jenny, the other child I chose for the task, was older than Susie and was not afraid of her, even though Susie had managed to bully quite a few of the other children. The initial results were disastrous. The two girls ended up pulling hair and fighting each other. However, I was persistent in trying to work with them both and I told the teacher I would not give up.

The following day the girls and I tried the same task once more. Again we had very bad results. At that point, I decided to invest some time in building a relationship with Susie. I borrowed several dolls from my own daughter who had outgrown them and brought them to the classroom. I told Susie that she could play with the dolls and perhaps even have one if she treated the dolls properly, with respect. I showed Susie how nicely I spoke to the dolls, and we invented names for them. The change in Susie's behavior was almost remarkable. Susie liked the game very much and began to treat the dolls with respect.

The next day, I gave Susie the suggestion that she treat her friends the same way she treated the dolls. I showed her how I treated her friends, and I suggested that we go back to the original task of completing the picture with Jenny. Susie was able to do it this time. Now I suggested to the teacher that Susie and Jenny, plus one other girl that Susie could not intimidate, become a group to do other tasks in the classroom. The teacher asked them to clean the blackboard. This time, there was almost no difficulty in accomplishing the task.

To further test my theory, I asked the teacher, several days later, to take one of the girls from our group and replace her with another girl whom Susie usually intimidated. This time, Susie was so focused on the task that she had no problem sharing with the other girls.

Though there is no clear method to teach pro-social moral behavior, if the focus is on interaction and relationship rather than punishment, even with children who are less intellectually gifted, we can achieve good results.

I emphasize my experience with Susie because, in my experience with older delinquents, those with lower aptitude prove to be very difficult to rehabilitate. In such cases, I believe that the real problem is not so much rehabilitation but habilitation. Those delinquents who seem hopeless and are likely to spend the rest of their lives in jail never received intensive and proper moral and social education when they were young children! If they did, in my opinion, like Susie, they too, would be capable of moral behavior.

If educators and parents are taught this method, I believe we can detect and prevent criminality in many young problem children before they become antisocial budding criminals. One way would be to introduce systematic teaching of pro-social behavior in nursery school, emphasizing respect for peers and adults, empathy, giving, sharing, helping others, and consideration of others. There is considerable evidence in research that children can get high on power, but they also can get high on helping others.

I remember taking my son at age two to the old age home run by my mother. Many of the residents suffered from Alzheimer's disease and often could not find their own rooms. My mother got great pleasure pointing out how well she trained her grandson to take the old people to their rooms and even help get them settled. The old people seemed to enjoy very much the interaction with this young child, and furthermore, my son was very pleased at how much he was helping the older people.

Young children learn mostly by doing, and doing for others can become a habit. However, they also learn by imitation.

Bart, a six-year-old boy, was referred to me by his school principal because Bart was disrupting the class. He was noisy, very oppositional, unable to sit still for more than five minutes and acted like a bully at recess, beating up smaller children. The teacher also suspected that he was stealing from other children, even though Bart was never caught. As a consultant at the school, I felt that I should get in touch with Bart's parents to see how he was behaving at home.

Sure enough, my suspicions were verified. Bart was caught several times stealing from toy stores and grocery stores, and he had been doing this, according to his father, since the age of three. Bart's mother tended to minimize the problem, stating that all kids steal on occasion. I felt Bart's problem, despite his young age, was serious.

Applying my preventive method, I rated Bart on the seven warning signs and was not surprised when he scored sixty. As could be expected, his highest scores were on low frustration tolerance and stealing, but his scores were also high on all other traits. Since self-centeredness seemed to be Bart's major problem, I felt if we focused on his self-centeredness, other traits would naturally be reduced.

Bart's parents were invited to the school, and with the teacher we decided on a common strategy to be applied both at home and at school. We attempted to focus mainly on reducing the seven traits systematically, one at a time. To start with, all activities involving Bart not being self-centered were immediately encouraged and enforced (not negotiable). For instance, if Bart was given ten candies, he would have to share them with his younger sister or classmates.

At school, Bart was required to assist and cooperate with the children in his classroom—primarily, the children he had been bullying. Any time he was caught hurting another child, Bart had to sit with the teacher and design a strategy on how to help the hurting child for the next two weeks. If Bart was caught lying or stealing, he was severely punished and required to help the person he stole from as well.

Bart's father was very cooperative. A week into the treatment, he advised me that Bart had stolen a truck from a toy store. We arranged to meet with the store manager, and Bart was required to help clean a section of the store to make amends for his stealing. We also attempted to use my empathy treatment where Bart's father and mother would consistently show how much Bart was hurting them.

Whenever Bart demonstrated inappropriate, antisocial behavior, we focused on replacing the inappropriate behavior with appropriate behavior. I arranged for a monthly meeting to evaluate our progress. After three months, Bart's behavior became worse instead of better. Since Bart's teacher had been very cooperative, I wondered if the problem might be at home. Investigation of the home revealed there was considerable disharmony and tension between the mother and father. I believe that Bart was able to exploit that disharmony to the fullest.

Bart's father had said that the boy had been stealing since the age of three, so in a sense, we were dealing with a criminal at the age of six who had a three-year record. Since adult control is necessary in order to achieve progress with criminal children, I felt that control had to be achieved and no excuses tolerated. I discovered that Bart had considerable control over his mother, and she always made excuses for him. I came to believe there were two opposing camps in the home: Bart and his mother were on one side, and his father and sister were on the other. Bart's sister, age three, did not show any problems similar to those demonstrated by Bart.

Six months later, I still saw no results, and the family moved away to another town. I never heard from them again.

Most of the cases which I have presented had positive outcomes. I believe this success rate occurred because the method by which I treat delinquent children is one that can be easily understood. In fact, parents and teachers can be taught to employ the method with very little professional assistance. My experience with Bart may have been a failure for two reasons: 1) we could not get cooperation from both parents, and 2) we were already dealing with a rather experienced budding criminal at the age of six. This demonstrates how urgent it is to prevent the development of criminality by beginning moral teaching at a very early age.

3

Mistakes We Make
in the Name of Love

Parents, educators, social workers, psychologists and psychiatrists, I believe, all have good intentions. Yet, many do a lot of damage in the name of love.

The first error parents commit revolves around giving children conditional versus unconditional love. Erich Frohm in his classic book, *The Art of Loving*, suggests that a mother's love is unconditional while a father's love is conditional. Conditional love means loving your child if he or she meets your expectations, and withdrawing your love if the child doesn't meet your expectations. Depending on the family situation, these positions can be reversed.

Using Frohm's theory, if a child gets a C in school when the father's goal was an A, the child feels unloved because he has disappointed his father. The child must get top grades to gain the father's love. In the case of a toddler, if the child has a temper tantrum because he didn't get his own way or because his sister has a bigger ice cream cone, the father could withdraw his love, leaving the child feeling unloved. A mother's love, according to Frohm, is unconditional and generally remains unchanged even if the child has a temper tantrum or receives a C in school.

Another example which demonstrates the conflicting nature of parents' love might be a child who steals a chocolate bar from the grocery store and comes home with it. The father reprimands him for stealing, takes him back to the store, and makes him apologize. Then he sends him to bed at six o'clock instead of his regular bedtime of eight o'clock.

On the other hand, the mother might instead say, "Well, Johnny is only four years old. What's the big deal of stealing a chocolate bar when he's cute and I love him very much?" Sending that message to the child is very confusing because he is obviously getting two messages, one from the father and another from the mother.

When dealing with budding criminals and antisocial children, the issue of conditional versus unconditional love is a lot more complicated. The budding criminal or antisocial child is an expert in taking advantage of family conflicts. In the experience just recounted, the child will obviously choose to side with his mother. The more he goes to mother, the more he is alienated from his father. The irony of this situation is that values can be taught only if the parent has control. This mother's interpretation of unconditional love can lead to almost total loss of control, while the father's interpretation of conditional love can lead to total alienation or separation between the child and the father.

The problem is not with the concept of unconditional love, but with the interpretation of it. I do not believe that conditional love is a good way to raise a child in any situation. Parents using conditional love, whether father or mother, produce a very insecure child. I call this the yo-yo principle. A child feels lovable if he meets his parent's expectations, unloved if he does not. In this case, he can only meet one parent's expectations. Unfortunately, this inconsistency can lead to development of a neurotic, disturbed child.

Unconditional love is misunderstood. It does not mean that the parent approves of undesirable antisocial, criminal behavior. The message to the child should be very clear: *I love you no matter what, but I don't like what you do sometimes.*

When she was three years old, my daughter picked up a half-empty glass and drank some beer. Afterward when we caught her, she became quite rude to her mother. My relationship with her mother at that time was far from ideal. It would have been easy to side with my daughter, as do many parents in unhappy marital situations so that they can appear to love the child more than the other parent. Nevertheless, I made it clear to my daughter that I did not approve of such bad-mouthing of her mother, yet I still loved her. Whenever I reprimanded my daughter, I was always very affectionate at the same time and never withdrew my love. Not to confuse her, I reinforced the reprimand with some form of punishment, yet at the same time I repeated how much I loved her. The most effective punishment for her was to remove something she liked. Regardless of my reprimands and punishments, my daughter told me she has never felt unloved. I believe this because I express my love for her not so much through words, but through actions, such as touching, hugging, and playing. I believe this is a good example of unconditional love.

No child, but particularly not the antisocial child, should be faced with ambiguity. Unconditional love always should be practiced and, at the same time, undesirable behavior should never be tolerated.

The second error parents commit in the name of love is to confuse loving a child with teaching a child how to love. The antisocial, potential criminal will use parental love as another way to boost his already inflated ego. He will only become more egocentric the more you love him in an unbalanced manner. That is why I suggest you should never make him feel better than anyone else. Never allow this type of child the opportunity to practice excessive self-love, a common mistake being taught and practiced by many professionals in the psychology field.

If we make mistakes in loving a non-criminal child, such a child will probably still turn out all right. Yet, with a potential criminal child, such mistakes can lead to disaster.

When dealing with a budding criminal child, the punishment for undesirable behavior at a very young age should be immediate and severe enough to make it clear to the child that antisocial behavior will never be tolerated. Yet, as soon as the punishment is over, the parent should encourage activities that will facilitate loving others through sharing, helping and giving. Refusal from the child to participate should result in another punishment.

Another common mistake occurs when a defiant child engages in undesirable or antisocial behavior and the parent tells the child she's "bad." If you repeatedly call a child "bad," she will start to believe she is bad, and her future behavior might conform to what she believes about herself.

A parent should never label a child as "bad," but should discriminate between the behavior and the child: *You are good; your behavior is unacceptable.*

A fourth common mistake made by parents in the name of love is making excuses for the wayward child, that is: *he is stealing for attention; she is screaming because she didn't get her own way and she is very sensitive; we should be more responsive to his needs; she is breaking rules and regulations because she is unique and she should be handled with care; he is a difficult child and doesn't get enough love because I'm at work all day and the baby-sitter doesn't love him; the nursery school teacher is stupid because she does not realize she is dealing with my special child.*

The poor excuses fall into several different categories. The most common type is rationalization, whereby a parent rationalizes the child's behavior by giving him either medical, sociological, or psychological excuses. Medical excuses are: *He has a lot of energy* or *He was a premature baby.* Sociological excuses usually refer to environmental deprivation: *She is stealing because we are poor and we can't afford to buy her what she wants, and she sees other children with these things.* Psychological excuses are: *He is disturbed because he does not see enough of his father* or *She is jealous of her brother and sister.* The more we provide excuses for a child with budding criminal tendencies, the more we contribute to his or her potential criminality.

Another common excuse used by parents in dealing with problem children is denial. Parents refuse to acknowledge there is something wrong with such a child. If Jane pulls her sister's hair, the parent calls it a normal situation between sisters. What the parent fails to see is that pulling hair is a symptom of many other maladaptive or antisocial behaviors. It is a warning sign.

Projection is another common alibi. Generally, this means

seeing the world from your perspective. It is a theory of psychological defense mechanism developed originally by Sigmund Freud and his daughter, Anna. In the case of the antisocial child, projection is demonstrated by the parents seeing the child as they wish to see him, rather than as an independent, different human being. If someone criticizes his or her child or sees the reality of the child not as the parent pictures the child to be, the parent rationalizes, denies or makes other excuses to avoid the reality of the situation.

The most common expression of projection is blaming: *the teacher does not understand my child; his peers are mean and rude; the world outside is very tough and I have to teach my child to be a fighter.* There is even a song entitled, "You and Me Against the World." Such thinking is a good example of projection.

Generally, I find that the more insecure the parents are, the more likely they are to use excuses to explain their child's budding criminal behavior, rather than teaching the child to take responsibility for his or her actions.

Here is a typical scenario: I taught some neighborhood children, ages three, five and seven, how to play soccer. I played with the three-year-olds against four of the older ones. We had been playing for a while when I noticed the mother of one four-year-old standing at the side watching the game. Her child grabbed the ball in his hands just in front of the goalie. I had already explained to the children that this would result in a penalty shot.

The rest of the children were more than willing to accept this rule, but not the child who grabbed the ball. He started screaming and protesting that if he did not grab the ball I would have scored a goal. When I placed the ball on the field for a penalty shot, the mother walked onto the field, grabbed the ball, gave it to her child and made fun of me, saying, "You are really a big man, beating the children at soccer."

I attempted to explain to her that if we changed the rules in the middle of the game, we couldn't call the game soccer. I tried to say it jokingly: "You might invent another game, but it's not soccer." At that point, the mother took her son home, complaining about my coaching style.

Teaching a child not to play by the rules is a very good way of teaching that child how to break the rules to suit himself. This is also a good example of a parent practicing denial. In fact, when that mother left, she said, "You should be ashamed of yourself. He is only a child."

A follow-up several years later of this child demonstrated he showed great talent in sports such as soccer, football and baseball, yet he was thrown off every team he played on. The seed for that behavior could have been planted by his mother, in the name of love.

Not long ago, a nursery school principal telephoned me to advise me that he saw bruises on Carrie, a little four-year-old girl. When he asked her twin brother about them, the boy denied any knowledge of the bruises. I suggested the principal should immediately contact the Children's Aid Society. A social worker called me to assist with the investigation. I invited the parents to the interview.

The twins were being raised by a single mother with a boyfriend. There was some evidence of abuse of the little girl. Initially, we suspected the boyfriend had administered the bruises, but after further inquiry of the children, it turned out that the twin brother was the instigator and this had been going on for some time. When we approached the mother with the problem, she at first attempted to blame the boyfriend and even stopped dating him. The boyfriend was devastated and denied it vehemently. As a result of the meeting, the Children's Aid Society took both children into custody.

In spite of a number of meetings with me and the Children's Aid Society representative, the mother refused to accept our findings that the girl's twin brother was abusing her. I explained to her that unless we faced the truth and started to treat the boy, she would not get her children back from the Children's Aid Society. She still refused to accept our findings and insisted that the twins liked and protected each other. I told her that is not the case when you are dealing with potential criminals. She responded, "I'm going to look for another psychologist,"—one, I realized, who would accept her version of the situation.

This case is another dramatic example of denial in the name of love. The mother was protecting her son and blaming an innocent man rather than facing the truth about her child and his behavior.

Like parents, professionals such as social workers, teachers, psychologists and psychiatrists may have good intentions, yet they sometimes make serious errors, also in the name of love. When a child starts acting out or showing oppositional behavior and lying and stealing, the concerned parent will often take the child to a professional. The general attitude of most professionals is to look into the behavior of the parents or the environment in which the family lives. They are looking for causes rather than checking to see what kind of child they are dealing with.

If a child starts stealing from the grocery or toy store or his mother's purse at the age of three or four, the most common hypothesis advanced by professionals is that the child is stealing to gain attention. They do not see that the potential criminal child is stealing for personal gain and fun!

A common scenario occurs when a single mother has a new boyfriend. Professionals frequently associate the child's stealing with jealousy because now the mother's love is divided between the child and the boyfriend. I would suggest that the child who steals would rather get away with it and avoid the attention, rather than doing it for attention.

Almost every juvenile offender I have talked to over the years has told me that they started stealing at a young age and kept stealing because they were very successful at it. It also gave them a sense of power and excitement. If they had been caught and appropriately punished every time they stole something, they would likely have stopped. You don't continue to put your hand on a hot stove if you get burned every time.

You can use the same rationale for violence and, at times, sadistic behavior. A bully in nursery school or first or second grade does not always get caught because adults don't see him and other children are too scared to tell on him. He is an expert enforcer, employing fear to maintain his power. Failure to understand these children frequently leads professionals in the wrong direction, because they look for causes or reasons for the child's misbehavior outside the child, instead of seeing them in the child.

We don't always have control over the environment of the child, yet we know that even young children are free to choose. If you provide a child with the opportunity to choose the right course (by the means discussed throughout this book), then the choice will most probably lead to the development of morality instead of the destruction of morality.

The most common mistake professionals make is assuming that neurological or medical problems are the cause of the child's misbehavior. One popular diagnosis for acting-out behavior and/or violence is Attention Deficit Disorder (ADD). It is true that a child with this disorder is hyperactive and has difficulty attending to tasks for any period of time. She seems to always seek excitement and shifts from one task to another. Yet, I observe many such children in my clinic, and I notice they are quite able to maintain attention if they find an activity they enjoy. For example, many of these children do well in sports that require a strong ability to be focused. However, the same children cannot focus in school. An overlooked reason, I believe, is that these children simply do not find school exciting enough.

In the name of love and professionalism, many educators and professionals fail to see that the most important thing to teach children is values. If they have the right values, Attention Deficit Disorder may inhibit learning, but will not deter children from becoming very good, responsible children.

Many children with ADD do not become criminals. Even so, there is a correlation between Attention Deficit Disorder and later criminality. I argue that ADD is certainly not the cause of it.

A very popular term in social work and teaching is *self-esteem*. Low self-esteem is used as an excuse to explain a child's failure in school. It is often suggested that children with low self-esteem will seek avenues to increase self-esteem such as violence, bullying, and getting high from lying and stealing.

Although I will discuss self-esteem in more detail later, I suggest that there is very little relationship between self-esteem and proper values.

Budding criminals generally do not have low self-esteem because, from a very early age, they get control of their homes, they have control of recess while at school, and they frequently take control of their classrooms. I suggest many times and in many ways in this book that references to *self-importance*, so popular among professionals, should be eliminated. It is focusing on *self* that helps promote criminality. Teaching antisocial children to love themselves and to have excessive self-esteem only feeds into their already overly inflated egos.

Psychologists dealing with young children usually stick to treatment called *behavior modification*. This approach is based on a learning theory developed initially with rats and dogs. My early experience using behavior modification with budding criminal children was positive, but only when it was used for a limited amount of time. While behavior modification apparently eliminates undesirable behavior, I have seen in long term cases that somehow either the behavior comes back or the children learn to hide their bad behavior from adults. The majority of professionals either do not understand the budding criminal child or fail to see that teaching proper moral values would be a more pragmatic way of reducing the problem. They also fail to see that a moral child is a happy child. Even toddlers seem happier when they are spontaneously helping others and sharing.

Budding criminals appear to be angry and certainly do not seem happy. I believe that part of their anger is due to their constant frustration because no one can satisfy their heightened needs for pleasure and fun all the time.

Another error commonly practiced by professionals, teachers and parents is based on a false belief that one must love oneself in order to love others. One professional gave me an analogy using money. He said, "If you have ten dollars, you can give eight away and keep two dollars for yourself, but you cannot give money if you don't have money. Similarly, if you love yourself, then you will be able to love others. If you have no love for yourself, you cannot love others."

My twenty years of experience with young and old criminals has proved to me that lack of self-love is not their major problem. Many are narcissistic and love themselves and because they are in love with themselves, they are unable to love others.

Some research suggests that a narcissist only appears to love himself but, in reality, he unconsciously hates himself. According to this theory, the narcissist needs to fill the vacuum of self-hate by seeking pleasure as a way of gaining love.

I have problems with this concept. I truly believe from my observations that if you give a budding criminal too much love, he will become addicted to receiving and slowly become incapable of giving. The concept of narcissism is not a very useful concept when talking about budding criminals, but common sense tells us that if you love yourself too much, there is no room for others. Also, if parents are instructed to facilitate self-love within their child as a means of enabling the child to love others, they will usually achieve the opposite results.

We know that a child is naturally egocentric. All efforts should be directed at reducing that egocentricity instead of increasing it. When you tell a child that he is better than anyone else, he starts believing it and then he may lose his connection with others.

Only a truly moral person can truly love. Love is not a state of mind, it is a process and activity. The more you engage a child in such activity, the more you teach him or her about love. With toddlers, such activity mainly involves sharing, giving and doing work projects with other children, rather than competing.

A five-year-old girl named Judy was brought to my clinic by her father, a single parent. Judy's mother was a prostitute and a cocaine addict who spent most of her time in jail. The court had awarded the father custody of the child.

Judy was extremely cute, and she certainly knew it. At the age of five she was playing with makeup and wearing grown-up clothes, some of which were inappropriate for a young girl. I noticed that the father made a lot of fuss over her, praising her as being smarter than anyone else and telling her she was beautiful and unique for a girl of her age. She was brought to the clinic because the nursery school teacher said she was impossible to handle. If she did not get her own way, she went wild. She told lies, she manipulated others, and the teacher was personally afraid, because one day Judy accused the teacher of hitting her. The child had even gone to the principal's office complaining about the teacher.

Judy's father was very protective, denying there was anything wrong with her. He insisted she was just more mature than other children and therefore needed special treatment. His only reason for bringing her to me was "because the school threatened to suspend her permanently if her behavior does not change."

As soon as I met Judy, I knew she'd been taught, because of her looks and intelligence, to love herself too much. There was no question in my mind that she would grow up to be a narcissist.

I thought Judy was an ideal candidate for the cognitive moral approach I utilize because she appeared to be highly emotional and in touch with her feelings, even though the feelings were self-serving. I asked her father to assess her in terms of our seven warning signs. I told him to evaluate her self-centeredness, lying, power and control, resentment of authority, low frustration tolerance, lack of empathy, and stealing.

When her father rated her, Judy scored high on all warning signs except stealing. Her overall score was fifty-four. Because she did not steal, her father did not believe that we were dealing with a budding criminal.

I spent considerable time trying to convince Judy's father that, despite the fact that Judy didn't steal, her problem was very serious because her score suggested that, if nothing was done now, Judy would have trouble the rest of her life. He finally grew prepared to listen and try my method.

The first thing I did was try to take control away from Judy. I explained to her father that as long as she had control at home and in the classroom, we would be wasting our time. I established a clear routine that Judy was to follow. Since it was quite a struggle to take control away from Judy, I offered her father all the help and assistance I could, even offering to go to their home to gain control.

Once we achieved control, I attempted to make Judy realize how much she was upsetting everyone around her. Initially, she did not seem to care. Yet she was very close to her father and loved him in her own way. I explained to her over and over how much he was upset and hurt by her behavior, using plenty of examples to demonstrate how she was hurting him.

I did the same thing simultaneously at the clinic. After establishing a relationship with Judy, I attempted to show her how much I got upset when she did not follow the established rules. I also provided Judy's teacher with instruction on applying my method and asked her to consistently follow that approach.

Two months later, we began to see some change. I believe the change came about because everyone involved with Judy—her teacher, her father, the baby-sitter, and myself—were consistent in applying the moral cognitive method. Once Judy started to demonstrate empathy towards her father and me, she started to show empathy towards other children in her class as well. At that point, I asked the teacher to start offering Judy alternative punishments such as time-outs, taking away privileges, or doing good things for the children in class she still hurt at times.

Because Judy was quite intelligent, she generally chose to help the children she hurt rather than accept the punishment. Eventually, the change in her was very significant. Judy became a leader in her classroom, and the teacher was very proud of her progress and change in behavior. Judy's teacher was so excited by my method of changing the behavior of manipulative children that she asked me to teach it at a professional development day to the whole school. Of course, I agreed to do so.

4

Warning Signs to Identify Young Problem Children (Up to Age Seven)

All parents wonder at times what types of people their children will grow up to be. Most parents aspire for their children to be successful and good. Yet some children grow up to be failures and evil-doers. Often parents then ask themselves, *Why? What did I do wrong?* With newspaper headlines filled with stories of children killing children, not only parents but society is asking the same questions. One in twenty children born today will spend some part of his or her adult life in a correctional institution. Crime of a violent nature by youths has risen 371 percent in the previous three decades.

I asked an adult criminal recently, "What would you do if your children followed in your footsteps as a criminal?" He responded, "I'd beat the hell out of them." Though his answer was crude, it is clear that even a criminal does not want his own children to follow in his footsteps.

Vast literature suggests there is a genetic factor in producing criminality. An equal amount of research shows that faulty upbringing produces criminality. However, from my long training and experience working with young problem children and young criminals, I conclude that we are obsessed with explanations. These are frequently tedious, mostly unproductive, and usually lead to the formulation of excuses and rationalizations rather than to the formulation of practical methods of change. In fact, I strongly believe this hyperbole comes too late. Our society does *not* know how to identify budding criminals. In fact, we do not invest any energy into identifying potential criminals, but we invest a *lot* of energy (and resources) into housing and supporting these individuals when they have become full-scale criminals.

If we are to stop children from becoming criminals, we need to be able to clearly identify deviant behavior early in a child's life and find methods to alter the risk factors to prevent development of criminality. We must deal with "how" to change deviant behavior rather than "why" it has occurred. Since certain behaviors give us warning signs, there are fundamental moral deficits that must be tackled and corrected earlier than later.

This subject has been my constant companion for twenty years. Since graduate school in the early seventies, I have been studying and working with young and old criminals. Like most psychology students, much of the training I received was of the traditional kind in which causes were sought for certain behaviors.

The rationale was, find the cause and you will be able to cure the behavior. I have learned that this is a naïve, unrealistic, and unproductive way to change the young criminal. Moreover, as I have painfully found out, it does not work.

During the past two decades, I have tried different methods to treat and understand the young criminal. Many failed. However, I believe I am now on the right track. Why? For the simple reason that juvenile offenders themselves tell me so. I do not claim to have a antidote for crime reduction. I simply want society to clearly understand what the warning signs of the young criminal are so that we may all be equipped to deal with the faulty behavior of these problem children before they act out violently. The best way to accomplish this is, first, to understand the characteristics of the young criminal. Shockingly, many of us will recognize children around us who are budding criminals.

Two simple principles of the origins of criminality appear to be contradictory but are actually complimentary: one, criminality, to a large extent, results from failure to effectively teach morality and values to the young; two, teaching morality and values must include the ability to make free choices. As I proceed through this book, it is my earnest hope that it will become clear that criminality is a developmental process which begins in early childhood. Environment rooted in community, peer groups, school and family plus individual poor choices interact to increase criminality. Those same conditions can, however, interact in the opposite direction. This is, I believe, the real foundation for change.

There is a red caution light for parents and others involved with teaching children when risk factors appear. However, the warning signs and bad behaviors of children are only significant and serious if they show consistency. All children rebel at times; all children show delinquent behavior at times—that's part of growing up. But, while non-criminal children slowly develop moral behavior by considering other people's rights and needs, potentially budding criminals develop in a different direction.

Budding criminals do not develop the natural tendencies that would enable them to survive as good citizens living in a law-abiding society. In fact, as they mature, they act out in more and more deviant ways.

These are the warning signs to heed:

Self-Centeredness

All children are self-centered. It is a requirement for survival. If a child does not cry when he wants milk, he may starve to death. Self-centeredness or egocentric behavior is normal in a child. Yet, most children, even very young ones, show some consideration and appreciation of others, as indicated by their capacity to share. Three examples illustrate this point.

My friend Elise has a son, Eliot, who is nearly two years old. Eliot shares candy and toys. In fact, I am always amazed at how much he is willing to share at such an early age. Unlike Eliot, the potentially delinquent child is almost totally egocentric. He will not share, because his wishes, desires, and needs take priority over others'.

Not long ago, I attended a party with twenty adults and about ten children, all of whom brought toys to the party. I observed Sandra, a girl of seven systematically stealing toys from the others and hiding them in a closet. Suddenly, complaints started coming from the other children—where are our toys? Sandra's mother must have suspected the theft might be her daughter's doing because I heard her ask her daughter, "Where are the toys?" Sandra denied that she had taken the toys. After several denials, the mother gave up. I went quietly to the mother and told her the toys were in the closet. The mother smiled with embarrassment, took the toys from the closet and returned them to the other children. She did not reprimand or talk harshly to the girl about such inappropriate behavior.

Another friend of mine, Joel, asked me to baby-sit his children until their mother returned home in order for me to evaluate some of the self-centered behaviors his children were exhibiting. I bought a twenty-piece bucket of fried chicken for myself and the children. The children were ages three, six and eight years.

The older child was in charge. I told him to ensure everyone received equal amounts of chicken—including his mother when she came home. I helped him with the mathematics, explaining that there were four pieces for each person. "But, I won't interfere," I said, "as to how you divide the chicken."

A few minutes later, upon checking, I found they'd left their mother only two pieces of chicken—wings with very little meat on them! I asked the children if they loved their mother and they said, "Of course we do."

Of course, not dividing the meal evenly with his mother could be just a childish action. However, when a child is self-centered in everything he does, it is not normal, and should be considered a warning sign.

Lying

There is a naïve notion that children do not lie. Of course, one must distinguish between a vivid imagination, which might be an expression of creativity, and deliberate lying used to avoid responsibility. We must realize that most children lie occasionally. The classic example of the child with his hand in the cookie jar illustrates this idea. When asked if he stole any cookies, he says no. Such examples of magical thinking and behavior are amusing and normal.

However, the potential criminal, even as a toddler, lies frequently, usually to avoid responsibility for some misbehavior. The three types of lies are: blaming others, lying to get what you want, and lying for no reason at all. Other traits found in children at risk from infancy include difficult temperament, impulsiveness and hyperactivity. *Even as toddlers and pre-schoolers, aggressive behavior, lying, and risk-taking are prevalent.*

Some examples bring this characteristic to life.

A brother and sister, Bob, age four, and Jill, age five, were left at the breakfast table. Jill spilled milk all over the floor. When her mother, Nancy, asked the children in a harsh voice who had spilled the milk, each pointed a finger at the other: "She did it." "He did it." Obviously, only one was lying. The mother punished them both, cutting television privileges for the evening. Nancy later told me, "This type of incident is very common."

Indeed it is. My friend Carla has two daughters, ages five and seven, and almost every time I visit, I see similar occurrences. Just as in the first example, these kids blame each other. Since I know the girls personally, I am quite sure I know which one is lying. Nevertheless, like Nancy, their mother consistently punishes both of them.

How does double punishment affect both children? Experience tells me it will produce resentment in a child who does not lie and disrespect in the child that does lie because she thinks, *My sibling is always getting blamed for something I have done.*

When I was about six years old, my classmates and I used Monopoly money to play games in mathematics class. One day, Todd, who was seven years old, asked the rest of the class to bring real money to class, promising to give us a lot more paper money. He managed to con the whole class and the next day each kid brought him real money. Indeed, Todd gave us a lot of paper money in exchange. However, when Mr. Sawyer, the teacher, realized what was happening, he asked Todd to explain. As expected, Todd adamantly denied any wrongdoing. He said that all of us had volunteered to bring money because we wanted the paper money that he had produced.

Mr. Sawyer prohibited us from playing with Todd for a period of a month. However, he never explained to us or to Todd, the promising con artist, the significance of the event. Thus, the teacher lost the opportunity to teach proper values.

Resentment of Authority

With a toddler, resentment of authority usually is expressed by his inability to tolerate the word "no." Whenever anyone says no to him, he reacts with temper tantrums, screaming and other oppositional behavior. Nevertheless, without rules and regulations, a resentful child does not develop discipline. For children to develop normally, parents must set rules.

This is easier said than done because the problem child resents rules and regulations. His parents may find it extremely difficult to teach him to accept discipline. As he gets older, there is constant struggle with parents, teachers and any person in authority. Unfortunately, I often hear parents of such children excuse the children's explosive behavior as an expression of independence rather than as a warning sign of budding criminals.

We have all heard small children cry and scream in shopping malls, restaurants, and other public places. If we pay close attention to events preceding this situation, it is usually the result of the child receiving a "no" answer in response to a request. A child may want candy from a store; she might want to eat ice cream rather than a regular meal; she might complain that her brother or sister has something bigger or better than she has. Whatever the case, it is usually a reflection of the child's inability to accept no from someone in authority. When this happens occasionally, it is normal.

However, the constant opposition to rules and regulations or to authority figures may explain why a child has difficulty from the first day at nursery school and later in elementary school. Conflict with authority figures such as teachers, school principals, and coaches signals "a rebel without a cause" behavior.

Control and Cruelty

Sometimes, by the age of two, a budding criminal child can be an expert in grabbing and maintaining control. He quickly recognizes that he can gain control by screaming, having a temper tantrum, sulking, lying, manipulating, and many other means. I once dated a woman with a three-year-old daughter who refused to go to bed, even if it was midnight, until the mother went to bed. In the struggle for control, the mother simply gave up and allowed the child to dictate her own bedtime because the mother could not tolerate the screaming. She also worried that people might think she was being abusive towards her child.

The explosive child learns early to use temper tantrums, aggression or manipulation to gain the power or control he or she wants. This is a behavior pattern leading to dire consequences.

The concept of a young child seeking and getting power and control of the family is an important one. I have seen hundreds of families with three- or four-year-olds essentially controlling their homes. If the child's attempts to gain power and control are always successful early on, the child can progress to more deviant forms of behavior as he or she grows more practiced and secure. Even in middle childhood, this can become criminal behavior. Schoolteachers can testify that bullies in the classroom exhibit such behavior. Bullies try to exercise power and control over anyone they perceive as weak. As they get older, bullies may be anxious to join gangs, with their ultimate goal being to gain more power and control.

The whole issue of sibling rivalry can be another area in which the problem child asserts power and control. All brothers and sisters will at times resent each other as they compete for parental attention. However, when this becomes a constant harangue between two or more siblings, great disharmony can arise in the family. The problem child may also exhibit jealousy in school where he may compete for the teacher's affection and in other activities where an adult's attention is essential, such as sports.

Lenny, an only child, was a very intelligent and handsome little boy. When he started nursery school, he initially became the teacher's pet as he was brighter than most of the other children. In addition, he received a lot of attention from his classmates because of his natural charm. One day, a new girl named Jenny joined the class. She was very cute, charming and entranced the other children with her ability to do ballet. To Lenny's dismay, Jenny very quickly gained popularity.

The change in Lenny was dramatic. First, he started to sulk, then he started to act out angrily towards the other children, primarily towards Jenny. When the teacher asked for my assistance, I observed that Jenny was essentially taking power away from Lenny and that Lenny's reactions were becoming more and more physical. I felt that if something was not done quickly and effectively, he could hurt Jenny very badly.

In fact, a few days later during recess, when Lenny had the opportunity, he tried to hit Jenny. However, he was not obvious about it—he was sneaky and lied and was difficult to catch.

One can go to any schoolyard at recess and watch small children at play. It will not take long to recognize potential bullies who consistently push and hurt other children. Many of them are also highly competitive and cannot stand to lose at any game, sometimes erupting in violence when they are losing.

Ed, another small child I counseled, appeared to be a polite child on the surface. His father, Frank, was a social worker and he had brought six-year-old Ed to my office because he would hit his mother whenever she said no to him. "One time," Frank said, "he even tried to stab her and Ed was only five years old then." The beating did not stop, even though the parents tried such disciplinary measures as time-outs and taking away television privileges.

Ed was never violent towards his father whom Ed understood to have greater physical strength. Budding criminals usually are smart enough to selectively use power and control. If they perceive peers or adults as more powerful than themselves, they will seldom challenge them. I suggested that, in Ed's case, the striking out at his mother was an assertion of power and control over the mother. This was already a serious situation. If drastic measures were not taken to correct the problem with such a child, violence might escalate toward his mother and develop towards women in general. Violence is an expression of a desire for power and control.

In addition to violence toward weaker human beings, in almost every case of a budding criminal you see the expression of power and control manifest through cruelty towards animals (usually cats or dogs). These kids seem to derive pleasure from hurting animals. They seem to get a high from the power, and that high is very addictive and leads to the children trying more ways to gain power over weaker people and creatures.

Low Frustration Tolerance

Budding delinquent children have very low frustration tolerance. If they want something, they want it *immediately* and will not tolerate any delay in the pursuit of fun, games, food, or toys. They perceive their surroundings, parents and others as objects for their satisfaction. Such children like people who can give them something and have no time for people who can't give them the things they want. If their wishes or desires are blocked or delayed, they become very demanding and often begin screaming and showing other oppositional behaviors.

One particularly notices such acting out in grocery stores or restaurants when a problem child is thwarted in his or her desires. He or she will scream and carry on and, in some cases, throw food or toys. Usually the child is quite successful in manipulating his parents to give him what he wants. After all, the parents also want to enjoy their meal or complete the shopping peacefully. Very early in life this child recognizes that public places are good vehicles for demanding behavior because parents are sometimes too embarrassed to resort to drastic methods to stop the inappropriate behavior.

Excitement

The budding criminal child is extremely hedonistic, always seeking pleasure and looking for fun and excitement. However, the fun and excitement he or she covets may or may not be at someone else's expense.

In the very young child (up to age five) this characteristic will not be easily distinguishable in recreational activities except in how he or she participates. Problem children, when playing with toys, will often break them (because they find this exciting) or move from toy to toy to toy, unable to focus on one for any length of time. The hedonistic child's tendencies toward seeking excitement are recognized, not only in coveting and being destructive with playthings, but in seeking undue stimulation from activities with his or her companions.

As these children mature slightly, the budding criminal likes to set up his friends to be punished. For example, John pretends his friend hit him and screams loudly with pain to his mother. John's mother gets very angry with the friend and threatens to ban him from visiting if the behavior continues. When his mother leaves the room, her son laughs and tells his friend, "I got you!"

Lack of Empathy

Empathy is generally defined as the ability to put oneself in someone else's shoes and to feel what the other person feels. Though the seeds of empathy are inherent, the development of empathy is gradual as children mature. However, some children seem to demonstrate a lack of empathy from a very early age. These problem children seem to be oblivious to the feelings of others. They are indifferent to the pain of others—whether they or someone else caused it. Such a lack of empathy leads some people to believe in the phenomenon of the "bad seed." Whatever its origin, the more this type of child needs power and control, the more he will lack empathy.

When such a child is caught hurting another child, he either denies it or blames it on the victim. Nursery school and first grade teachers tell me there are generally two or three children in their classes showing this specific trait. They hurt others, laugh at them, ridicule them, and when caught, either deny or blame the victim or make some other ridiculous excuse.

Nevertheless, I believe that children who show little empathy at early ages have the capacity to learn empathy because they usually do show some empathy towards those they love (mother, close friend, or sometimes a pet). However, the empathy does not develop as it does in a non-criminal child.

Empathy is one of the most important characteristics of human beings. The shift to doing the right thing because it is the right thing to do, instead of pursuing an action because of an external reward, can only occur if empathy is developed. Such development does not usually occur spontaneously with budding criminal children. It must be systematically taught.

Distortion of Love

Even at a young age, the budding criminal's concept of love is selfish. He only loves the people he can manipulate, use, or exploit. When such a child tells his mother, *I love you,* he only means, *Let's see what you can do for me, not what I can do for you.*

The problem child is almost incapable of sharing, whether it be food or toys, with siblings, peers, or parents.

When my friend Sam visited me a few years ago with his five-year-old child, my own daughter was six years old and my son was eight. I was a single father, and we had only four pillows between our three beds. Sam's young daughter, Erica, threw a temper tantrum when it was time to go to bed, saying, "I always sleep with two pillows." Finally, her embarrassed father gave in, giving her two pillows. This meant that either my son or daughter would have to sleep without a pillow that night. I decided to talk to Erica, patiently explaining that it was unfair that she had two pillows while my daughter volunteered to sleep without one.

While I was talking to her, she became angrier. Another temper tantrum quickly followed. Her father immediately came to her aid and told me to stay out of it. That was the last time Erica was invited to my home.

Lack of Responsibility and Discipline

Teaching responsibility and discipline to an explosive child is an immense task. His or her need for power and control continuously blocks the capacity to learn responsibility and discipline.

For example, such a child will not keep a promise and will ignore any kind of commitment. Being told to pick up toys or do simple chores after dinner or before bedtime means very little to such a child. He is an expert at making excuses for not doing what he promised to do.

I recently discussed the problem of responsibility with Carol Jones, a first grade teacher. She said that one thing she noticed about the problem children in her classes is that they hardly ever take responsibility for their misdeeds. Carol explained that children continually steal, lie, hurt other children, and disrupt the class and that they will rarely admit committing such acts, either making excuses or denying the misdeed altogether.

Discipline at young ages usually requires structure and routine. Disruptive children sabotage structure; for example, they disregard regular eating times, bedtimes, etc. It is always a big struggle to get them to do what parents ask because their main focus is excitement and fun.

Parents who consult me describe bedtimes for such children as disasters. Like the child of my date of whom I spoke earlier, they refuse to go to bed and scream for hours. They want to continue playing or sleep in the parent's bed. Parents frequently concede and give the child what he wants because the parents are tired of the constant struggle. Lack of responsibility and discipline in their first seven years will haunt these children for life. It may reappear again in their inability to keep regular employment or make commitments, or even more seriously, in the development of criminal personalities and behavior. No matter what the outcome, this is a long-term, not just an immediate problem.

Stealing

Theft is a common problem with disruptive children and it starts very early in the budding criminal. They steal chocolate from grocery stores, magazines from newsstands, and money from their mothers' purses at very early ages. They also often show keen interest in sex at very early ages. They do not feel guilty when they get caught, and surprisingly, the practice of having them go back to the store to return the goods does not have an effect on them. (This remedy seems to be very effective with most "normal" children though).

Mark, who spent many years in jail, gave me his story. Here it is in his own words:

My first "theft" occurred at the age of four. I was in the variety store with my mother, saw the chocolate bar behind the counter, went and stole it. Emotionally, I didn't feel guilty until I was sent back to the store by my mother. Then I was scared for myself, even though I had no thoughts or feelings of guilt insofar as the owner of the store was concerned.

At the age of six, my brother and I would break into parked cars—me at the wheel and my brother working the clutch and brake pedals. We used to coast the cars down the street and crash them. Once again, fear for myself but no guilt.

By the time I was ten, I was stealing money from the Red Cross glass jar where I and my classmates had been asked to contribute part of our allowances. What should be noted here was the fact that I did this alone and once again, during the process, I feared for my safety. I never was concerned about whom I was stealing from.

To me, at least the turning point or pivotal point was when I was eleven. I accompanied my father's live-in girlfriend to the local grocery store and fiddled with the combination lock on the safes at the front of the store and lo and behold, one of them opened up. The cashier rushed over and closed the safe as everyone laughed about it. She asked me to see if I could open it up again. During this moment, I felt a feeling of self-worth, a sense of accomplishment and I never forgot the experience of feeling important.

The following years were full of thefts and other petty crimes but during all this I cannot remember ever feeling a sense of remorse or guilt. It was normal for me to take what was not mine. Fear of being exposed was my only concern. I did not care about the victims of my acts.

As in Mark's case, what is really disturbing about stealing which begins in early childhood is that these budding criminals never show empathy or guilt about how much distress they have caused their victims. In fact, they usually show quite a bit of excitement about their endeavors and often brag to their peers about their stealing.

From the early age of three or four, such individuals will begin to build their self-esteem on different values than non-criminal children do. Being a successful thief is very important to the development of their self-image.

When I ask teenage juvenile offenders in jail to tell me when they started to steal, they almost all admit that they started such activity at the age of three or four. Because they were rather successful at it, even if they were caught occasionally, it certainly did not deter them from stealing.

Some experiments with animals suggest that if you reinforce certain behaviors some of the time, but not all the time, the behavior then becomes habitual. This theory certainly applies to budding criminal children and explains why such children become habitual thieves.

A friend approached me to see if there was something wrong with his four-year-old daughter, Gayle, who was throwing temper tantrums at home but not at school. At school, Gayle was polite, friendly, showed the ability to share and got along with others; at home, she was a brat. I suggested that there must be a weak link in the family that the child had managed to control. Since the father suggested the temper tantrums did not occur in his presence, it was rather obvious in this case that it was the mother.

This is an example of how a child learns to manipulate and control a parent. Could such a child become a criminal? Though manipulation of one adult is not as serious as the attempts to manipulate all, one should be very careful to watch the behavior of such a child when around an adult that the child can control or manipulate. The problem can be corrected once identified if the parent (in Gayle's case, the mother) is willing to cooperate.

I would like to reemphasize that demonstration of one or two of the traits I have discussed is not sufficient indication to suggest that a child may develop into a criminal. Only if we see most of them demonstrated should we be worried.

To be predictive of a budding criminal, it is also important to realize that these traits must show up in multiple settings such as at home, school, shopping malls, restaurants, playgrounds, etc. If the child shows some signs in one place but not another, it is serious but not as serious as if such traits appear in all places.

5

Hints for Reducing Budding Behavior in Young Children

The issue of power and control must be addressed and resolved early in a defiant child's life. Any advice by professionals (and I have heard and seen much) specifying that you should never get into a power struggle with your children is...bull! If you give toddlers and young children control, you not only ruin the child, but you also make your own life miserable. Why? Because the child will develop an irrational addiction to power. Whether or not that power is real or a delusion doesn't alter the result: a very difficult, troubled child who will go through life destroying social relationships with peers, authority figures, parents and eventually his own serious relationships.

Even with a dog, you are raising a potentially dangerous animal if you give it too much power and control. Jed, an acquaintance of mine, could not have visitors in the house, especially children, because his jealous dog would bite anyone who showed affection to the owner. Eventually, Jed spent a large part of his life alone. It was obvious the dog controlled the home.

How did that dog gain so much power? Simply, his owner let the animal have anything it wanted, any time it wanted, without any restrictions, and this produced chaos in the home. The same principle applies to children.

Too much power and control at an early age can and many times does produce a potential criminal. I cannot recall a single case of a budding criminal child in twenty years, when after an investigation, I did not find the most common factor to be a child who had control and manipulated their family at a very early age. In my findings, this single element is even more significant than the common argument that a child who comes from an abusive home will likely become an abuser.

Addiction to power destroys children, organizations, and countries, and ultimately, becomes one of the most significant influences in creating evil people and perhaps an evil society.

How does one gain control? Regardless of the setting—restaurant, shopping mall, stores, school, home—the adult in charge of the child—mother, father, teacher, or counselor—must establish control.

The parent who jumps every time the child cries creates a potential control problem. Generally, a parent can discriminate when a baby's cry is based on real needs, such as hunger or a wet diaper, as opposed to a cry based on wants, like wanting to be immediately picked up or to play with a potentially dangerous toy. Yet, as the child matures, I know many parents who still jump every time the child cries, giving in to whatever the child wants to stop the crying.

If parents have difficulty discriminating between real needs and wants, there are many books and counselors which can provide excellent training on that subject which will be useful with non-criminal children. However, the many books available on how to love a child, how to discipline a child, and how to raise healthy children don't apply to the budding criminal. Such books fail to understand that these are not normal children.

Because budding criminal children have already successfully gained power and control, parents will find it becomes almost impossible to teach them pro-social values without additional help. The child's needs, wishes, and whims have become more important than the feelings and reactions of the people around them.

In fact, the teaching of values and pro-social behaviors, such as compassion, empathy, respect, and consideration for others, is lacking in our present society in general. As for teaching these traits to budding criminals, we seem completely lost, although I maintain that this can be done. How? By repetition of key concepts.

When children have difficulty learning to read or pronounce words, we don't give up teaching them—we send them to specialists who have the expertise to help these children. When we identify a child who apparently has problems learning and developing pro-social behavior, we send him to specialists who apply standard treatment models such as behavior modification. Unfortunately, standard models don't work with budding criminals because behavior modification traditionally focuses on the resulting behavior instead of on regaining of control.

Many good teachers instinctively know what to do with these children while others are at a complete loss as to what to do. This is because the budding criminal is an expert in getting control, and he gets control not only at home but also at school and wherever else he might be.

Professionals who talk about the development of moral thinking in problem children usually identify those children as being stuck at an egocentric stage. They teach morality by rewarding good behavior and punishing bad behavior. The problem is the budding criminal will quickly learn how to outsmart this technique, and if he doesn't, he will simply resent being punished and become even more difficult to teach.

If a budding criminal is rewarded, we are feeding an inflated ego of a child who thinks she deserves it anyway. This is not the way to teach morality to such children. The teaching of pro-social behavior to children with budding criminal tendencies must be done by first gaining total control of the child. Once control is achieved, then you can progress to instilling values.

Bobby, age three, is taken to a grocery store and he just loves chocolate. His father refuses to buy him a chocolate bar, so Bobby throws a temper tantrum in the store. What can his father do to get control? Time out? Maybe. Refuse to give him chocolate?

Of course. What happens the next time they go to the store and the scenario is repeated? One key concept is repetition because bad habits die hard. Another is to learn to know the individual child who is exhibiting problem behavior. What works with one does not always work with another.

I have found that many problem children love affection and respond well to love and empathy. If you give such a child love and if you are empathic with the child, he will probably build a good relationship with you. Then he may try to please you because he is afraid of losing you. To achieve this result, you must make it worthwhile for him to be with you.

Young children love to play games and be the center of attention. The first step in getting to know a particular child's personality and finding out what processes work for changing his faulty behavior is to play games with him. However, the game must be played by your rules, rather than the child's. If he does not win, he may try to change the rules of the game. Don't ever let him do that. Once you establish a rapport, the fear of losing you is an extremely good motivation for the child to allow you to get control and play by your rules. Then new learning can begin.

My own children have always seemed willing to spend time with me, especially as babies, partly because they simply had fun with me. I was always able to play on the floor with them and at their level. I never tried to bring them to my level. I think one of the reasons I have been successful was that I truly enjoyed playing on the floor—I'm a big kid myself. Getting down to a child's level and playing his games is a good way to establish the necessary rapport for changing bad behavior. Of course, responsible adults should always distinguish between being childish and childlike. Childlike is very natural and healthy; childish is immature.

Many children in my clinical practice over the last twenty years have seemed to relate to me well. Because of this, I have been able to take control away from them. Because they enjoy being with me, respect me, and perhaps fear losing my attention, I have been able to gain control. Though fear is not to be used idly, and certainly not as a physical measure, the right kind of fear, as I've proven in *Tough*

Talk (about which I'll talk later), can be used by responsible adults for gaining control, especially in serious situations with budding criminal children.

Most books on effective parenting neglect the idea of the use of games and play to gain a child's respect and love. One thing I always emphasize when battling to get control from a child is that love is sharing. I share and the child shares. Love is always an activity in giving, rather than taking. I truly believe that too many parents, professionals and teachers are addicted to loving, rather than teaching the child how to love.

I must emphasize that the earlier you start to take control away from a manipulative child, the easier it is for you to do it. Remember, each child will respond differently. Some will respond best if you remove something they like. Don't despair if a particular child doesn't respond to a particular method. Trial and error is the process here. Some children, especially the types to throw temper tantrums, will respond best to time-outs. On the other hand, some will respond to the establishment of stricter rules. If you are persistent enough, you will gain control.

Loving a child requires three simultaneous processes: you must love him, empathize with him, and teach him how to love and empathize with others. When teaching morality to a budding criminal, the lessons should be focused on four main areas: empathy, love, discipline, and responsibility.

Empathy, as I've noted earlier, is the basic foundation for morality. A moral child not only understands right and wrong but also feels what is right and wrong—this is what I call true moral feeling. Without such feeling, values never become internalized and will always depend on external factors rather than internal ones. True moral feeling means I will share my toys or food with you, not because of what I will get out of it, but because it is the right thing to do—I will share for the sake of sharing.

Though much of my thinking on changing budding criminal children is the result of considerable experience with young delinquents and older criminals, a lot of my thinking on teaching children morals has been influenced by the intellectual feminist movement, primarily by Dr. Carol Gilligan, a teacher at Harvard University. Dr. Gilligan suggested that there is a difference between men and women in their concept of morality. While men view morality as an intellectual abstract concept, emphasizing understanding, women view morality based more on caring and empathy.

As Mary Maples Dunn observes in the *Radcliffe Quarterly*, "...recently the angle of vision has shifted to the broader study—that is, the attempt to define difference, whether constructed or innate, and to explore the social construction of appropriate roles for men and women, and their impact on individuals and society." It is in this context that we may interpret the differences in men's and women's viewing of morality.

In his book, *Emotional Intelligence*, Dr. Daniel Goleman, suggests that a child's emotional development and sensitivity is very much dependent on his emotional contact with his mother. According to Goleman, the mother's ability to empathize with the child along with mostly non-verbal communication during infancy, promotes development of empathy. Such development can only occur if the mother starts early enough to teach empathy to the child.

However, my own thinking, as I noted earlier, is that the potential for empathy is innate. Nevertheless, though innate, if it is not developed in the young child, the capacity for empathy will slowly wither away. The cost of failing to develop and teach empathy is devastating. Some of the most outrageous children's criminal activity—children killing children, abusing them, sadistic action towards other children—is the result of our failure to develop empathy in our children.

Another psychologist, Dr. Martin Hoffman, sees a natural progression in the development of empathy, initially towards the parents, usually the mother, siblings and peers, and eventually towards strangers. Again, I would like to emphasize that the failure to develop empathy may be the key to the development of criminality. Any treatment method ignoring empathy is like teaching reading without knowing the alphabet.

The *feeling* aspect of empathy is a key requirement for the internalization of moral values. Only if a child can experience the distress and the joy of other humans can he develop into a truly moral person.

Again, gender provides differences in the expression of empathy. A man will say empathy is, *I see what you feel*, whereas, a woman will say, *I feel what you feel*. In his book, *The Brighter Side of Human Nature*, Alfie Kohn quoted another psychologist, William Damon, who suggested "most scholars believe that moral emotions are a natural component of a child's social repertoire and that the potential for moral emotions and reactions is present at birth."

Several studies demonstrate that even babies and toddlers show distress towards someone else's pain, especially if they are responsible for that pain. The trouble with budding criminal children is that they have not developed this feeling, and, once it lies fallow, the question becomes, *how do you teach empathy to a budding criminal child?*

In my own practice, I have discovered that almost all children can be taught empathy. I would argue that the concept of psychopathy, being without conscience, in children is very rare.

Whenever a child is brought to me for treatment because he steals, lies, disobeys adults, and is aggressive, my first task is to gain the child's respect and make sure the child likes me. Building a relationship with a problem child may be made easier because many of them strongly desire approval. Once this rapport has been established and a strong relationship develops, such a child will generally want to please the adult. At this point, the child is still externally motivated; responsibility comes later.

But let's remember that stealing, lying, and aggression are all behaviors the child does which hurt other people, usually the parents and eventually other victims. We need the child to realize that he has inflicted hurt. As a counselor, I am persistent and ask the parents to also be persistent in showing the child the effects of his behavior on them. Sooner or later he will make the connection between his hurtful behavior and the effects on his parents. In other words, if the child who comes to my clinic is hurting his brother or sister, he may not be too concerned about the emotional or physical pain he put his brother or sister through. However, he will usually be upset if he sees his parents or loved ones getting upset.

Constant repetition of the process of allowing a child to see the results of his or her negative behavior on those he or she loves generally produces positive results. This means the child himself now starts to internalize the pain of someone else. He begins to empathize.

The younger the child, the more amenable he or she is to moving from external to internal motivation. For this reason, I like to catch these children before five to ten years elapse and rehabilitation is necessary. As long as the criminal is still budding and is not full blown, habilitation is possible.

It has been my experience that, if the adults involved with a problem child consistently use the approach of habilitation, empathy begins to develop. The best thing you can do with a child who is exhibiting the warning signs of a budding criminal is to let him or her see and feel your tears when you are upset.

I would like to emphasize that this only works if you have a good relationship with the child. If the relationship is strong and the child truly loves you and can feel for you, he needs your approval. If the child resents you or dislikes you, your tears will achieve the opposite results.

One child who was brought to me for counseling was Michael, a six-year-old. Because Michael was often acting out aggressively, his parents were afraid that he would hurt his newborn sister. In fact, they had already caught him sneaking into the infant's bedroom and hitting her. All traditional approaches of teaching Michael that he should respect his new sister did not seem to have any effect on him.

During my investigation, I found out that Michael was also beating up children at nursery school, throwing temper tantrums when not getting his own way and seldom, if ever, taking responsibility for his actions. Furthermore, he was making excuses and telling lies. Both parents and teachers were at a loss as to what to do. The social worker felt that Michael was jealous of his new sister and that was why he was aggressive towards her. This may have been the case, but it did not explain why he was stealing, beating up other children and constantly lying.

I gave Michael's parents a copy of an article of mine, "Warning Signs," and told them to give a copy to the school. I asked them to define Michael's behaviors in the future in terms of the warning signs. The school principal telephoned me the following day and told me that the boy exhibited all of the warning signs. It was obvious to me that we were dealing with a budding criminal and traditional methods would not work with such a child.

For the first three months at my clinic, I spent most of the sessions trying to establish a relationship with Michael. Finally, his mother told me that Michael had started to talk about me all the time at home. At that point, my empathy training began.

Deciding to use the *distress method* to develop feelings of empathy within Michael, I asked Michael's mother to come to the session and produce tears, telling Michael how much she was upset by his hitting his sister. I used my own acting ability to show Michael that I was emotionally distraught over his actions, and a few times his mother and I cried together. At first, Michael looked puzzled at our behavior during these sessions, but very soon I noticed that he started to bring me toys or candy every time he came to the clinic. Once the behavior changes began, it was evident that the rudimentary foundation of empathy had been established.

We then contacted Michael's teacher, asking her if she noticed different behavior in school. The teacher reported that even though Michael was not showing distress in regard to others' pain, his aggressive behavior had almost totally disappeared.

To further develop Michael's moral feelings, I suggested to the teacher that instead of punishing Michael and sending him to the office when he acted out in a defiant manner or harmed another, she should sit with him and design a program where he could help the child who was hurt by his behavior. It took another three months, but Michael became a teacher's helper. He not only started to do good things for others, but he wanted to help the teacher as well. The transition from getting high on power tripping and other young criminal behaviors to getting high on positive acts started to happen. Michael was now receiving self-satisfaction from doing good.

Part of the reason for getting good results was the cooperation from the school and a principal who believed in the effectiveness of my method. I am not claiming that the distress method I used with Michael is the only way to train problem children to internalize values. However, whenever I have achieved good results, it has been when such an approach was used consistently and persistently by all adults involved. I have also found that sometimes the resistance to this approach comes from professionals rather than the child's family.

Once you teach empathy, the child will then feel guilty if he does harm to others. It is the feeling of guilt which the child begins to focus on others, rather than expecting others to feel guilty for him. In effect, this guilty feeling helps initiate changes in a problem child's behavior, as I will discuss later in the book.

How do you teach love? Just as one must ask, *How do you teach empathy?* In dealing with budding criminal children, the question of teaching love is equally relevant. We know that the budding criminal's concept of love is based on *what love can do for me* and never *what I can do for love*. Parents sometimes think that by loving their child they will automatically teach him or her how to love. This is not generally so. Even with a toddler, love needs to be taught. Simple messages are best: giving is better than taking, sharing is better than keeping for oneself. But once a child shows risk factors, teaching love and sharing is no longer simple.

My father had a very interesting concept of sharing. I have spoken to many teachers, parents, and professionals, but no one has heard of my father's concept of sharing. If I were given a choco-late bar and shared half with my sister, my father would reprimand me. His concept of sharing was to take one-third for myself and give my sister two-thirds of the chocolate bar. I cannot recall once when I was allowed to share equally. Forty years later, when I still share my father's way, it always brings a smile to my wife's face. I would truly feel guilty if I were to divide something only equally.

Though it must be actively demonstrated rather than taught by example, even the budding criminal child, because of his or her need for approval and love, can be taught to share. I recently talked to a first grade teacher who told me that she very seldom sees chil-dren share toys, food or whatever with others. In the Old Testament, one example of love was the sharing of the cloth. In the New Testament there is the example of Jesus sharing the loaves and fishes. Perhaps we should teach our little ones that sharing should be a routine activity and one can share even with people we do not necessarily know or like.

Another example of how to teach loving behavior is to take a four- or five-year-old problem child to a retirement home or a school for mentally challenged people and teach them to help those less fortunate. I asked a father not too long ago to take his daughter, Stacy, who was showing some serious warning signs of risk behavior, such as lying and cruelty, to an old age home where many people had Alzheimer's disease. Stacy's job was to guide an elderly woman to her room and stay and talk with her. Stacy, who initially demon-strated an inability to share and had very egocentric behavior, sud-denly began to change. She actually enjoyed helping the older peo-ple and they enjoyed her; she gave and she received.

Doing volunteer work can start at a very young age. When a child starts to help others, his attitude changes and self-cen-teredness is reduced. The more self-centeredness is reduced, the more likely the child will begin to develop pro-social values such as caring, loving, compassion, and respect for others.

I have worked for several years in a school for the blind and noticed that children with some sight are always willing to help those who are totally blind, at any age. One cannot engage in helping behavior and hurting behavior simultaneously. The replacement of one behavior by another can begin even at the very early ages of three and four.

I recently browsed through a large bookstore and was amazed at how many books there were on disciplining children who behave badly. While some experts on discipline do give good advice, the problem with the discipline approach with the budding criminal is that discipline alone will not work until you first teach a child who is acting out in a deviant way the importance of values. If you apply discipline through fear or punishment, you only produce a more clever budding criminal. Many problem children will appear compliant while you watch, but when you're not looking, they will engage in even worse oppositional behavior.

As Ronald Moorish said in his book, *Secrets of Discipline*, "Certain things are not negotiable." Many parents make the mistake of frequently negotiating the rules and regulations that bring structure to a child's life—i.e. going to bed, cleaning the room, picking up the toys, and other chores—such rules are non-negotiable. As soon as you negotiate, you lose control. You may find that once a child starts to develop good values, you do not need to negotiate any more. Children will come up with their own good ideas.

You will recall my baby-sitting episode where twenty pieces of chicken were divided among three children and two adults and how the mother was allotted two pieces instead of four. In this case, it should be explained, using the ideas of sharing, that giving the mother four pieces is an expression of love.

Remember another example I used of the two siblings, the spilled milk and the mother who punished them both by depriving them of their favorite television program? Such blanket punishment will only lead to both sisters resenting their mother, especially the child who did not spill the milk. An alternate method of resolving the conflict would be to sit in front of the girls and tell them that if the guilty person would admit the truth, she would not be punished for it, but would get a reward for being honest. In other words, do not punish the innocent party—both children should get special rewards for doing the right thing.

In my example of my own childhood experience with the Monopoly money, all the children in the class gave one boy, who was already experienced in conning his peers, real money for paper money. The punishment given by the teacher to the con artist was so severe that he was not allowed to talk to anyone for a full month. I suspect the damage to that child was irreversible.

As I noted, the teacher had not only punished inappropriately, but missed a perfect opportunity to teach all the children in the class good values. He should have discussed with the con artist that the proper way to deal with the problem was to return everyone's money. It was also important for the con artist to think of some way he could do a favor for the rest of the class. Such a resolution of the problem would be much more productive. The con artist is not alienated from the rest of the class, there is restitution, and the teacher would have used the opportunity to develop moral feelings by showing the children how to help others.

In my research of authorities' theories on discipline, I have again discovered that most people who advise parents on how to discipline children do not recognize when they are dealing with a budding criminal. I have seen highly disciplined children and adults who are dangerous criminals.

Think of a soldier who kills an innocent person, claiming he was following an order. He is a highly disciplined individual but certainly not moral. Young children who belong to a gang at a very early age, some as early as ages seven or eight, can be quite disciplined within the gang's code of ethics, yet are they moral?

Webster's Dictionary defines discipline as "teaching self-control." Self-control is very important in teaching children that they cannot have everything they want, whenever they want. However, a budding criminal who plans to steal toys from a store or money from his mother's purse is not out of control. He knows exactly what he is doing and he likes doing it.

When talking about responsibility in regard to a budding criminal, the most important thing is to dismiss all excuses for irresponsible, hurtful, immoral behavior and to reward only for responsible behavior. If you combine the teaching of responsibility with discipline and emphasize that certain behavior is correct and some is not correct (that kind of behavior is not negotiable), then you, the adult, are always in charge. As mentioned previously, if you first have a good relationship with the child and then teach the elements of responsibility, you will, in many cases, eventually achieve the desired result—self-responsibility.

William Glasser in his brilliant book, *Reality Therapy*, defines responsibility as "the ability to fulfill the child's needs in such a way as does not deprive others of their needs." Similarly, an irresponsible person will pursue his needs frequently at other people's expense.

For example, if a child wants or needs his mother's love, it does not mean that when his sister asks for love, he should push his sister away so that he gets it all. Nor should he manipulate his mother so that she feels if she does not give enough love to him, he will become disturbed.

Furthermore, Glasser suggests that all moral behavior stems from accepting responsibility. Irresponsibility leads to emotional sickness; responsibility leads to moral and healthy human beings. As I believe, he emphasizes that responsibility and accountability can only be taught in the context of relationships. If you attempt to teach responsibility without having a good relationship, the child will only build resentment and sabotage anything you teach. Or, if he is physically afraid of you (the wrong kind of fear), he will pretend to listen and, as soon as you turn your back, he will do the opposite.

I cannot stress enough that in all my counseling experiences with problem children, I tend to get good results only when I have a good relationship with the child I am seeing. If you treat children with respect, they will treat you with respect, provided, of course, that you have the control.

Glasser also suggests that children will only develop normally if their needs are satisfied. Parents or educators must explore the possibility that a child's inappropriate behavior may be a reaction to some basic need that is not being satisfied. For example, if a child goes to school in the morning without breakfast and is tired and irritable the rest of the morning, this is not delinquent behavior—it is simply a response based on the frustration of being hungry. Any sensitive adult will learn to discriminate between behaviors based on needs and those used as a means of manipulation. Sensitivity is paramount in dealing successfully with all children. It is especially important in dealing with children showing signs of budding criminality.

Finally, if for one reason or another the adult applies all these methods and the warning signs of a budding criminal are still evident, I suggest that parents, teachers, or professionals should systematically try to tackle every warning sign. Since self-centeredness is the primary factor in the development of a budding criminal, all activity reducing self-centeredness must not only be encouraged but continually reinforced.

Self-centeredness and lack of sharing in budding criminal children may be seen in major and minor incidents. Both should be corrected since the first usually leads to the second. If a child refuses to share his bicycle with his sister, he might be told that he will lose his bicycle altogether, and then it should be taken away from him for a period of time until he is willing to share it. Similarly, if he is not willing to share a chocolate bar with his sister, take the chocolate away from him. Perhaps a few days later, you can try again.

Lying should never be tolerated. A four-year-old toddler does not understand the concept of lying to spare someone's feelings—white lies. A small child usually lies to avoid responsibility, blame someone else for his misbehavior, or gain control of a situation. If Johnny hurt his sister by hitting her and then lied about it, he should be punished twice—once for lying and once for hitting her.

Again, I would like to emphasize that punishment is not very effective with problem children because it gives them an excuse for further misbehavior. However, rewarding a child for good behavior or for telling the truth will sometimes eliminate the need to punish the child.

Another important trait is resentment of authority.

Resentment of authority by a toddler is usually expressed by temper tantrums or screaming when he is told "no." This should also be systematically eliminated. Remember the three-year-old daughter of the woman I was dating who refused to go to bed at an appropriate time? Her mother was afraid that the child's screaming would somehow hurt her and, after a half-hour of screaming, the mother would give in. I suggested to the mother that we should allow her daughter to scream and not give in. The first night the girl screamed for five hours straight. The second night she screamed for three hours. The third night she went to bed almost immediately—no screaming. After one-half hour, her mother was very curious to see what her daughter was doing. She was sleeping like a baby.

The budding criminal gets excitement from having power over others. Stealing, violence, and torturing animals are very exciting. He or she should be taught to get excitement from helping others. With proper guidance by a responsible adult, he will learn to feel satisfied by doing helpful and moral activities rather than hurtful activities.

Kevin was a very strong boy in second grade who constantly beat up other children to gain control of the class. He really liked the teacher, but I learned from checking his background that he had very little love and empathy at home. I advised the teacher to spend more time with Kevin and try to build a relationship with him. Whenever Kevin was caught doing hurtful things to another child, the teacher sat with him and together they designed a program of helping that injured child.

It did not take long for the teacher to notice a change in Kevin. Before he was power-tripping on hurting children; now he was power-tripping on helping children. In fact, he was truly excited about the possibility of helping. He also became a teacher's helper, wanting to clean the classroom at the end of the day and always thinking of things to do to please the teacher.

This type of shift can occur if the child is young enough and if he is sufficiently dependent on adults for affection and love.

Another risk trait that is dangerous—stealing—should

never be tolerated. The standard technique of asking a child to return the chocolate he stole from the grocery store and apologize to the owner has limited value. By the time parents catch him, the budding criminal has usually stolen so many times and gotten away with it that he can tolerate the discomfort of returning an item the one time he is caught. A better method involves asking the child to pay for the chocolate by working either for the grocery store or by doing some other helpful activity at home or at school. He should then return more than equal the value of the goods to the store owner.

Many budding criminal children get their apprenticeship in stealing at home. If you catch a child stealing at home, instead of punishing him, make him do chores or perform service activities for the benefit of the family. Although this sounds harsh, harsh measures are called for to rehabilitate a budding criminal child. If the child refuses, make his or her life more miserable than the alternative—doing chores—so that the best choice is clear.

There is no clear-cut method for achieving rehabilitation of a problem child who has a high degree of warning signs of potential criminality. You must use trial and error. It is important to try several techniques to get control back in your hands so that the rest of the teachings can follow.

Not long ago, I was called in to help a teacher with Barbara, a five-year-old kindergarten girl who was consistently disrupting the teacher's class. Barbara was an attractive child and very intelligent but seemed to show all the traits of a budding criminal—self-centeredness, lack of respect, lying, inability to tolerate "no," and stealing from other children. I contacted Barbara's parents and discovered that her father was a truck driver who was hardly ever at home, and therefore, the mother had primary responsibility for raising the child. Her mother told me she had to hide her purse and jewelry because they were constantly disappearing. Obviously, Barbara was practicing stealing at home. Although the school reported incidents of theft, the girl was clever enough not to get caught. Her mother was very disturbed and wanted to find a method of dealing with the problem before her child became a full-blown criminal.

I might add that Barbara was also caught stealing from a grocery store and her mother made her return the goods to the store and apologize to the store owner. All of the methods Barbara's mother had tried failed, and the stealing and anti-social behavior were increasing instead of decreasing.

I made a point of going to their home to observe interactions between Barbara, an only child, and her mother. Almost immediately, I noticed that she negotiated with Barbara on almost every task or chore. It seemed clear that I had to teach Barbara's mother to take control away from the child in order to initiate responsible behavior. Can a five-year-old show responsible behavior? Absolutely.

After observing the girl for a while, I noticed she was very fond of certain television programs and one particular toy. Her mother had tried to use time-outs as a form of punishment with very little success. In fact, she was afraid her daughter might hurt herself by the way she always carried on in the time-out room.

I suggested that we remove Barbara's favorite toy as a way of getting control (behavior modification) and stop negotiating. "We have a crisis here," I said. "Total control must be achieved at all costs." At that point, I realized that perhaps we could obtain control if we used the empathy training which I advocated earlier. Since the girl was very much attached to her mother, I asked the mother to show Barbara how upset she was every time the girl did something that hurt her. I also spent considerable time trying to build a relationship with Barbara, consistently showing the same distressed emotion at Barbara's bad behavior as her mother. Whenever Barbara did anything to hurt her mother, rather than punishing her, we asked her to think of something she could do to please her mother. Moreover, we asked Barbara to come up with some ideas for good deeds for her teacher or another classmate at school.

I showed the teacher in the school the same techniques of facing the child and showing her how upset she was. Initially,

Barbara did not respond to the empathy training either at home or school. Yet, she seemed to like devising ways to help other children, so we focused on that. I also insisted that every day Barbara had to find something to share with me, her mother, teacher, and other children in school—candy, a toy, etc. When Barbara at first refused, her favorite toy was removed. This upset her greatly.

By consistently applying these methods, the stealing almost totally disappeared as well as the lying. Unfortunately, we were not totally successful though in eliminating all aggressive behavior. I suspect Barbara tended to bully other children and they were afraid to tell.

However, good results were apparent in Barbara's new, more responsible, and caring behavior. A follow-up with the mother suggested that the violence also disappeared. This was largely the result of her mother consistently demonstrating her own hurt whenever Barbara misbehaved. Again, encouraging the child to do good deeds for people she hurt (responsible behavior) seemed to change the negative behavior. Essentially, we systematically taught Barbara to replace the immoral behavior of hurting other children with the moral behavior of helping them instead.

6

Good Children, Bad Children, and Dangerous Violent Children

Everyone knows what a *good* child is. Such a child likes to share; he is friendly; he shows compassion and consideration for other children and adults; instinctively he knows what respect is and he respects people and animals; he is a happy child—honest, charming and lovable. When such a child does something wrong, he feels guilty and hardly needs to be punished for his misdeed because the guilt itself will provide him with incentive not to repeat the act.

The good child hardly needs to be taught empathy—he is naturally empathic about other people's pain or joy. By our definition, this child is not very self-centered and he seldom, if ever, would have fun at someone else's expense.

What is a *bad* child? He is abusive, aggressive, angry, argumentative, belligerent, callous, cold, crude, cruel, deceitful, devious, dishonest, extremely egotistical, ignorant, manipulative, obstinate, offensive and, at times, violent and anti-social. Will such a child become a criminal? Not necessarily.

There are many concomitants which combine to make a problem child into a criminal, and only some escalate into criminal behavior. However, in a lot of cases a child's behavior reveals what he will be like as an adult. If we review the criminal adult's character as a child, we find that risk factors of bad behavior were operative from age four to seventeen. Nevertheless, often these children are resourceful enough or lucky enough to have someone make excuses for them so that they seldom, if ever, get into brushes with the law.

There is also a group of manipulative adults who, as children, have personalities similar to those of children who become criminals. These individuals come from good homes and achieve success in their lives by becoming doctors, lawyers, businessmen, university professors and skilled tradesmen. Nevertheless, they lack moral education. Unfortunately, though successful in their professions, they spend their lives alienating everyone around them. I strongly believe that even though as children they did not end up in jail, group homes, foster homes, or as wards of the state, they lacked moral fiber and were never systematically taught values.

Part of the reason for their later successes may be based on the fact that many are grandiose. They think, and always have thought, they are special and better than others and are highly motivated to prove how special they are. They think only of themselves and are totally self-involved.

At times, psychologists may define them as narcissists, people in love with themselves. Many narcissists are successful in life but throughout their lives leave victims behind.

One of the basic differences between narcissistic children and young criminals is that criminals turn to crime because they are failures, whereas narcissists are driven to succeed at any cost and usually do, especially if they are intelligent. Parents or teachers who knew these individuals as children probably didn't find them lovable. Such children only shared their knowledge, or other things in their possession, if there was something in it for them. They never did good deeds for the sake of doing good.

Later, because of their grandiosity and successes, narcissistic adults are very difficult to deal with and change. Because they have control of their lives and the lives of those around them, you cannot take control from them. They either have power that is real, or they are a legend in their own minds.

Another significant difference between these grandiose individuals as children and the young criminal is that most grandiose children are cowardly. Fear is a great motivator for them. Even though they may show some of the same traits as the budding criminal, they are too afraid to get into brushes with the law. On the other hand, the young criminal is usually motivated by power, fun, excitement, and living on the edge. Young criminals seem to exhibit more courage than grandiose children, even though this type of courage leads him or her in the wrong direction.

When grandiose individuals are children, I define them as "bad kids." They use their resources to do damage within the system, rather than against the system. Since grandiose children won't relinquish control, and surrendering control is the basic ingredient for change, we fail to change these bad kids when we try. Even if we actually wrest control away from such a child, he does not believe that we have done so and may behave even more inappropriately.

Grandiose children are seldom referred to professionals for counseling because they usually do well in school and in sports. It does not appear to bother them that no one likes them. They feel superior to others and pretend they don't need anyone, only needing others to use and manipulate. They never look at others as equals or friends.

Many grandiose individuals are smart enough to wear disguises. When we meet them, they can be very charming. Because their true identity is usually concealed, we never know what they are really thinking. Only if we study them carefully do we realize that their masks cloak the truth of their deviant personalities.

Another group, even more destructive and frightening than grandiose individuals are those who, as children, may be described as *dangerous and violent* but mask their real selves. In addition to the standard traits described earlier as part of the personalities of grandiose children, dangerous children exhibit another feature which in degree is different from the traits of other problem children and grandiose ones. They are extremely callous and cold, and they show no ability for empathy. Like full-blown psychopaths, they are malicious and enjoy inflicting pain. From a very early age they look for excitement; they are hedonistic and self-indulgent with no consideration for anyone else. They consider all people, both other children as well as adults, as objects to be used and manipulated for pleasure.

Dangerous children seldom associate with those who understand their true personalities and they are keen in locating victims. What makes them so dangerous to society is that almost all of them are very angry behind their disguises. This anger, in fact, is overwhelming, and if you study them carefully, they exhibit rage through their body language and attitudes, despite their masks of civility. Their anger, however, is selective. They realize the advantage of being superficially charming, especially when threatened. Their selective anger is designed to intimidate, and the older they become, the more menacing they become. In a fertile climate, those showing power-stricken attributes as teenagers will become leaders of gangs. Others with weaker attributes will become followers in gangs. Both spend their lives in fantasy worlds dreaming of unlimited money and freewheeling lifestyles.

One way that we can detect what children who mask their dangerous and violent real selves are really like is by watching how they relate to other children and animals. They are sadistic, gaining pleasure from hurting. Their inability to feel empathy will eventually turn many of them into rapists, violent criminals, and potential killers. Should we fear them? Of course, we should.

If we evaluate the risk factors of bad behavior for *dangerous and violent* children, which I detailed earlier, it will show the most extreme examples. Some budding criminals may exhibit 20 percent of the risk factors, some 50 percent, but dangerous kids show 100 percent—100 percent being the extreme of the traits. Is there a quality of difference between them and other young criminals? I believe so.

The majority of young and adult criminals are not malicious, nor do they wear masks. They do what they do for self-interest. Dangerous and violent children are also motivated by self-interest.

Theirs, however, is often sought at someone else's pain and they enjoy it.

Psychological literature usually defines a dangerous and violent child as a young psychopath. Hervey Cleckley in his book, *The Mask of Sanity*, suggests that such children are really insane even though when we first meet them they appear perfectly sane.

Ted Collins, a colleague of mine, adopted a child a few years ago. This child was extremely violent and would viciously taunt and abuse his dog. He even attempted to sexually assault his younger sister. When he was brought to me for counseling, I used the cognitive moral approach, as suggested in this book. I got nowhere.

I suggested to the father that this child showed signs of having a psychopathic personality, and I advised him that he would have to watch his son all the time. I truly believed that we were dealing with a very dangerous child. The father took the child to see other professionals who drew the same conclusion.

The last time I spoke to Ted, he told me that he had returned the boy to the adoption agency. I don't know where this child will end up, but I believe he has the capacity to eventually kill or rape someone and will probably spend a significant portion of his life in jail.

A child like that is relatively rare. Yet, we have seen increasingly more of them over the last few years. A telling example earlier referred to is the two young boys in England who beat a toddler on the railroad tracks and left him there to die. As well, the young boys who shot their schoolmates and teacher in Arkansas, committing these acts apparently because one of the boys was rejected by his girlfriend, are examples of dangerous children. I suggest that if you check the backgrounds of such children carefully, you will see all the warning signs I have earlier described.

Peter Reinharz, chief of the New York City Prosecution Unit, in his book, *Killer Kids, Bad Law: Tales of the Juvenile Court System*, provides us with many chilling examples of children similar to those I have discussed.

One particular case stands out. A boy named Johnny Rogers reports that after committing violent crimes, he never feels remorse. He explains that he enjoys the hurt and pain he inflicts on his victims. By the time Johnny was eight years old and in the third grade, he had already been suspended from school for fighting. Johnny's mother could not control him, and from the age of nine he used to stay out until three in the morning. His aggression continued to escalate, and he was arrested for possession of an electronic stun-gun. He also consistently stole money from his parents and smoked marijuana. He told a psychiatrist that he carried a knife and that he used this knife in several fights. He almost died at the age of twelve when another youth grabbed the knife and stabbed him. He refused to tell the psychiatrist how many people he had stabbed over the course of his short, but violent life.

Around the age of thirteen, Johnny was arrested for beating another boy so badly that the boy almost died. When asked why he did it, Johnny said, "The kid was messing with me and he deserved to be killed."

Reinharz talks later in the book about four youths on a subway train having fun by trying to scare everyone on the train. The four youths focused attention on a young couple sitting in the middle of the car. They had no idea that the couple was on their first date. The youths started by saying, "Hey, what are you looking at?" followed by racial remarks.

Suddenly one of the youths yelled, "Do it!" In an instant, the innocent young man was thrown from his seat to the floor of the train. The four youths kicked him about the head and body. When the man cried for mercy, the excitement of the attackers increased. Since the victim was wearing glasses, one youth drove his boot with a steel toe through the lens of the man's glasses, sending shards of glass into his eye. As the train pulled into the next station, the four youths ran from the car laughing.

The youths did not take any property—this savage act was not about stealing. Their purpose was simply to gain pleasure from the pain of their victims. Their violent actions were done for recreation and entertainment purposes—they were just having fun.

In another particularly vicious incident, eleven- and twelve-year-old boys attacked a woman with a baby in her automobile, raping the woman viciously. One youth held the two-year-old child in the back seat, covering the baby's mouth; the twelve-year-old had a gun and laughingly pointed it towards the woman as he raped her. When the youths finished their attack, they drove the car for a distance and then shoved the woman and child into the street.

Unfortunately, there are too many similarly violent incidents today. The important thing to realize in these cases is that we are dealing with a small percentage of children, who from a very early age exhibit a lack of compassion, empathy, and many other human qualities that most people exhibit. Remember, the way we can recognize such children is by watching their enjoyment of the power they have over their victims. Rather than showing remorse or guilt, they show excitement and consider hurting another human being as fun.

Hervey Cleckley, in *The Mask of Sanity*, suggests that these dangerous children are beyond treatment and will inevitably grow up to become adult psychopaths. The best we can do is to try to achieve some control over them.

Even so, I am not willing to give up on them. I suggest that the best way to deal with such children is to gain total control over *every* aspect of the wayward youth's life until responsible behavior begins. All people involved with these kids should be informed as to the kind of violent personality with which they are dealing. They must appeal to the child's self-interest, show that all violations will be severely punished, and never accept any excuses, recognizing that lying is a way of life for this type of child. The counselor dealing with a dangerous child should make sure that the youth knows and understands the new rules completely and accepts that he can't disobey or overpower the counselor.

In my own experience with young criminals, I make sure that control, especially in an institutional setting, means the youth not only likes me but is also afraid of me. Fear, as I've said before, can be an effective means of controlling such children. Because these children are extremely hedonistic, the necessary control may be achieved by depriving them of fun for any kind of infraction. The fear must be positive and have more to do with loss of privileges than physical fear.

Frank, a young client of mine was confined to an institution where I worked as a consultant. He was four years old when his parents brought him to the institution. His parents could not control him. When they said no to Frank, a temper tantrum always followed. When they put him in a time-out room, he would become enraged and try to destroy anything around him. If they put him in a room with no furniture, he would then try to hurt himself.

Frank seemed to feel no pain, nor did it bother him when he was bleeding. When he first came to the institution, he was evaluated by a psychiatrist and a neurologist. The psychiatrist felt that we simply were dealing with a spoiled child. The neurologist found some abnormality in the brain, yet it was difficult to explain Frank's behavior using the neurological data.

As I studied Frank and sought ways to help him, I found that Frank rarely spoke even though he was quite intelligent. I was involved with him for three years—sometimes seeing him once a week, other times once a month. Frank liked me because I was always able to engage him in games he found challenging. Around the age of six, I started to teach him chess. Frank liked the strategy of the game very much and played well for his age.

Frank was very aggressive towards other children and was extremely jealous if I paid attention to another child. He demanded that I see him every time I came to the institution—he became absolutely wild if I did not set aside the time to see him.

As I continued to work with Frank, I noticed he did not steal from other children but derived great enjoyment from hurting them. Frank always denied his violence, even when he was caught. Moreover, punishment following his aggressive behavior seemed to have no effect on him. It made him even angrier and more violent. The most effective means of control I used was to deprive him of the games we played together, an act which greatly disturbed him. I also used this method at times to reinforce his proper behavior.

What I found remarkable about Frank was that there was no affect—no feeling. He operated almost like a machine. There were no signs of remorse or guilt for his actions. Even when he got excited, his response was bizarre—laughing in an almost sarcastic way. I almost got the impression Frank was laughing at us. He truly enjoyed it when I made a fool of myself playing games; for instance, if he won the game, he would rub it in. Yet he always wanted to play games with me. Even if he lost the game, he wanted to play again.

As Frank got older, he became more violent and abusive, not only towards his peers but towards staff members. He had to be isolated. At times, he was even put in a straight jacket. Frank was also receiving heavy medication in an attempt to tranquilize him, with some moderate success.

Since Frank was extremely strong for his age, some of the staff were afraid of him. On one occasion I was called to the institution because Frank had become very abusive. He had been put into a straight jacket and was spitting food at the staff and carrying on like a wounded animal. At that point, I decided to resort to something very radical. I closed the door, making sure no one saw me, and I put my face close to Frank and pretended I was possessed by the devil. I then made peculiar sounds like the ones in *The Exorcist* movie. The change in Frank was dramatic. The spitting stopped. The aggressiveness stopped. I noticed that he was staring at me in fascination and fear.

Although Frank's violent behavior did not completely cease, I believe that I was able to achieve some control of Frank only by using psychological fear. I used the threat of removing myself from his life to instill fear in him. Though my seeking him out reinforced his feeling of being special, in his own mind, he could not decide whether I was his friend or enemy. That uncertainty provided me with control at least sporadically, so that we could get some measure of cooperation from Frank. However, our goal to make him a civilized human being who was not a danger to society was not realized.

There is no easy way of dealing with children who seem to show no moral fiber. I call them kids with *moral deficit*. With such children, only limited rehabilitation appears possible.

In another case, I counseled two girls with moral deficits, Diane and Mary. On the surface they appeared very much alike. Both were twelve years old and both had been placed in an institution for emotionally disturbed children because their parents could not handle them. Both girls exhibited extreme behavior problems usually demonstrated by oppositional behavior, temper tantrums, aggressiveness, and stealing, although I soon found that Diane acted out more than Mary did.

I began to establish a rapport with Mary and our relationship improved very quickly. She trusted me, she liked my company, and we spent a lot of time together playing games, going for walks and talking. Her good behavior with me, however, did not seem to carry over with other people. She was still very aggressive with her peers and other members of the staff.

One day, I took Mary and several other girls on a trip in my car to a recreational park. Having a weak stomach, Mary vomited all over the car. The other girls screamed at her and were very annoyed. I patiently cleaned up the vomit and reassured Mary that I still loved her. She walked a few steps away from the girls, looked at me, and started to cry, telling me that if I loved her that much, she must be worth something. I began to cry too and hugged her.

That experience seemed to facilitate a dramatic change in Mary's behavior. She began to relate better to her peers and other staff. A few months later her behavior had changed significantly enough that she was able to leave the institution.

Five years later, I found Mary's telephone number in the Toronto phone book. I was curious how her life had progressed, so I called. She told me that she had gone to college, had a nice boyfriend, and planned to get married. Although she sounded friendly, she did not want to see me. Perhaps she did not want to relive the experience of the institution.

On the other hand, Diane, who initially appeared to be less of a problem child than Mary, was charming and friendly on the surface with me. She seemed much older than her twelve years. After two months of working together, she began to act and speak flirtatiously. When I asked her why she had started to behave that way, she said she had been doing it since she was six years old—and was very successful at seducing many men, including several doctors.

What was remarkable about Diane was that her charm and social skills were nothing but a means of manipulating people to gain favors. She further told me that she never exposed the men with whom she was involved, but used sexual favors like blackmail. She received money and jewelry from many of the men. In other words, she learned very early in life how to get what she wanted through manipulation.

Diane did what she did for profit, and the men involved with her were, in my opinion, fully responsible for what they were doing. Yet, no amount of therapy changed Diane's behavior. Out of desperation, I referred Diane to a female therapist for further treatment, hoping that would help. Without change, Diane's sexual promiscuity continued—she showed no remorse, nor did she want to change. When discussing her case with other colleagues, we arrived at the same conclusion. Having begun her sexual apprenticeship at six years old, Diane would likely end up as a prostitute.

I suggest that the basic difference between what I consider dangerous children and good children is not always apparent, yet one class of children does not feel good about doing bad things while the other does. Perhaps there lies the difference between possible good and real evil.

7

A Day in the Life of a Budding Criminal (Age Twelve)

Jim hardly ever knew his father, who left when Jim was four years old. The warning signs described in chapter four certainly fit Jim. He was always oppositional; he reacted strongly to the word "no"; he had difficulty getting along with other kids in nursery school; he showed violent behavior, bullying classmates at a very young age; and to outside observers it was obvious that he had control of the house.

Jim's mother, a single parent, tried her best to raise Jim to be an honest, moral child, but with very little success. Jim was now in seventh grade and was quite intelligent but, even so, he had difficulty all through school.

Each morning, Jim got up at eight o'clock and rushed through his breakfast so that he could catch a bus at eight-thirty to go to school. Jim never sat at the front of the bus—he usually managed to get a seat in the back, away from the driver. One day, Jim was in a very foul humor because he did not like his breakfast. His mother was out of his favorite cereal so instead, she prepared eggs, which he hates.

It did not take long before Jim picked a fight with another boy at the back of the bus. At school, his first class was English. After twenty minutes of grammar exercises, Jim became bored and started throwing paper airplanes at the teacher. It took the teacher several minutes to realize who was doing it because there were many problem kids in the class.

When the teacher confronted Jim with his behavior, Jim immediately blamed it on Johnny, his friend who sat next to him. Johnny was not passive and within minutes the boys started hitting each other. This disrupted the class and both boys were sent to the principal's office.

The principal told the boys that it was apparent Jim was the instigator and did not believe Jim's lies. He warned Jim that he would be thrown out of school if his disruptive behavior continued. Jim promised to behave for the remainder of the day and returned to his classroom.

Within a half-hour, Jim started fighting with Johnny again. He was immediately sent to the principal's office for the second time that day. The principal decided to suspend Jim from school for one week and called his mother. Advising her of the situation, the principal requested, "Please pick him up." His mother had to get special permission from her employer to leave work.

Since Jim's mother had to return to work and didn't want to leave Jim alone, she called a sitter. Jim behaved for about an hour while the sitter fixed him lunch. Immediately after he finished eating, he disappeared while the sitter, who was only sixteen, was cleaning up and did not notice that Jim was missing. Jim wanted to meet his friend Jason in another part of town but he had no money for bus fare. He noticed a bicycle a few blocks from his home with a combination lock. Being an expert at breaking locks, he went back to his garage for tools, picked the lock on the bicycle, and rode off to see his friend.

When he arrived at Jason's, the boy told Jim that there was a new neighbor nearby with a dirt bike. "The bike's sometimes left unlocked in the garage," Jason explained. The two boys then went to the neighbor's house to see if they could steal the dirt bike, which only took a few minutes. Soon the boys were off laughing with excitement and driving the dirt bike through the neighborhood.

A short time later, the boys left the bike a few blocks from Jason's home, deciding that it was time to party at Jason's. Jason had managed to steal a bottle of vodka from his father's liquor cabinet and the two boys decided to have a few drinks. Jim always had a supply of marijuana, which he kept in a safe place in the basement of his home. He figured he could easily get it. However, he knew that the sitter was probably looking for him by now.

Jim went home, cased his own house and noticed that the sitter was cooking something in the kitchen. That provided Jim with the opportunity to sneak through a basement window, pick up the marijuana, and go back to Jason's house to enjoy a smoke.

Meanwhile, the sitter was frantic because she was unable to find Jim. She tried to call his mother at work, but she was in a meeting. Around three o'clock, the sitter finally reached her. Jim's mother rushed home and began looking for Jim. When she didn't find him nearby, she surmised that he might be with Jason, whom she'd told her son not to see. Driving to Jason's home, she barged in. As soon as the boys saw her, they tried to hide the marijuana but she had already smelled it.

Telling Jim to get in her car, his mother drove him home and attempted to punish him by depriving him of all television privileges. "Your bedtime for the next month will be seven o'clock," she yelled. Surprisingly, Jim went along with the punishment. He went to bed and when she checked an hour later, he was asleep.

At that point, Jim's mother went to her room and tried to relax, not realizing that Jim was only pretending to be asleep. Within minutes of her checking up on him, he snuck out of the house to continue partying with his friend Jason. Exhausted from her hectic day, Jim's mother fell asleep, not realizing Jim had left the house. The partying went on at Jason's house until midnight. Jason's parents, who were busy partying themselves, were not very strict and didn't mind the boys staying together until midnight.

Around midnight, Jim returned home, snuck through the basement to his bedroom and went to sleep. When he woke up at eight the next morning, he had an incredible hangover and pretended to his mother, "I must have picked up the flu from another kid at school." Since Jim had already been suspended from school, she left him at home once again with the bewildered baby-sitter. And the cycle began again. Without intervention, Jim is well on his way to a full-blown life of criminality.

8

Middle Childhood and Preadolescent Problem Children (8 to 12 Years Old)

Our discussion of the risk factors of bad behavior during infancy and early childhood shows that such traits as impulsiveness, aggressive behavior, and lack of guilt or empathy often emerge early in the problem child's life. According to a recent report by the Office of Juvenile Justice and Delinquency Prevention's Study Group of Serious and Violent Juvenile Offenders, children who display many of these traits are five to twenty times more likely to become violent young criminals.

It is important to understand that, as the problem child moves into middle childhood and preadolescence, his or her budding criminal behaviors often intensify and expand. Among the risk factors that are seen in middle childhood are: stealing and general delinquency, depression, sexual activity, and widened exposure to violence. When coupled with other risk factors such as poor parental supervision, below average academic achievement, and truancy, these factors set the stage for criminality to flourish.

In dealing with preadolescent problem children between the ages of eight and twelve, we must realize that since preventive strategies were not employed when they were younger, we are now facing a more serious level of defiance. I would like to emphasize that while warning signs in this age group may be similar to the younger age group, behavior is considerably different.

Budding criminal children between the ages of eight and twelve have learned that, because of their young ages, there is very little the law can do to them. This lack of fear encourages five common criminal activities. The first and most frequent is stealing—they steal from their mothers' purses, from other children, grocery stores, variety stores, and from the streets. Many are opportunistic and seldom let an opportunity for thievery pass.

Both girls and boys steal money, but they also steal objects specific to their gender. A boy may steal a leather jacket or blue jeans from a store or a bicycle from the street. Girls will shoplift makeup, perfume and jewelry.

The second most common criminal activity in middle childhood is assault. At this age, children, especially boys, begin to fight. Since most of them are in middle school, many of the fights occur on school property during recess or after school.

Third is vandalism. Ricky, an eleven-year-old criminal, told me that he and his friends used to steal screwdrivers and then go to a parking lot at night and unscrew car headlights, just for fun. Vandalism may also occur at school (breaking furniture, computers, etc.)

Setting fires is very popular among criminal children in this age group. Minor cases of arson include burning garbage disposal bins and trash cans. More serious cases involve setting fire to homes, garages, schools, and barns.

Finally, budding criminal children in this age group start to commit break and enters. You will see that break and enters are more common in the next age group of budding criminals, but defiant children's apprenticeships for these crimes start here. I might add that some of these youngsters, especially those in gangs, may be doing break and enters for older youths or even adults. An older criminal might use younger children because police can do very little to punish them. In exchange, the children get a percentage of the profit.

Budding criminal children from eight to twelve also start to show excessive interest in sex. Many sexual stories they tell are fantasies though, as some of them do not seem to have the nerve yet to take action. They also may explore homosexual activities; however, this is the exception rather than the rule.

At this age, young delinquents also start experimenting with drugs and alcohol and may quickly end up addicted. The most popular of these drugs are marijuana, cocaine, hard liquor, and beer. Furthermore, since much of their criminal behavior occurs in school, many of these kids get suspended frequently. They do not view this as punishment—rather they are excited about it.

Many young criminals who have the opportunity, especially those from lower socio-economic environments, also join gangs when they are between the ages of eight and twelve. Their motivation for joining gangs is mainly the money, excitement, and power obtained from gang membership. A child belonging to a gang is capable of more outrageous crimes than a child that operates on his own. Being a member of a gang also gives a child a sense of being protected by the gang. Joining a gang may be relatively easy compared to getting out of it. In many instances, when a child tries to drop out, the whole family is forced to leave town because the child is in danger of the gang's retaliation.

Children who join gangs are frequently insecure. The power and control that the gang can provide compensate for this insecurity. I asked Bob, an eleven-year-old criminal, why he wasn't in a gang. He told me that he wasn't a wimp—"I can do crime alone, and I don't need any protection from them."

Many young criminals of this age who operate on their own or with only one partner fear gangs but do not necessarily respect them. (In the criminal subculture, fear is frequently confused with respect.)

The major characteristics of young criminals from eight to twelve years old are very similar to the crimes committed by other age groups, however there are some differences. Also, the behaviors by which they exhibit these characteristics vary because of their age.

Low Frustration Tolerance

The eight-to-twelve-year-old criminal seeks as much fun and pleasure as possible. Generally, by middle childhood he has already successfully designed ways of getting what he wants. Parents and especially single mothers have often given up disciplining the young criminal by the time he or she is eight or nine years old. They don't want to fight any more and generally just give in.

Low frustration tolerance may explain why these defiant children seldom do well in school. Even when in class they will look for ways to create excitement through disruption rather than tolerate listening to the teacher for the duration of the lesson.

Ben was a ten-year-old problem child referred to me by his father, who described Ben's risk behavior of violent rages and destructive tantrums to me. I concluded that Ben was exhibiting signs of low frustration tolerance. His father recalled that, when Ben was four, he began throwing temper tantrums when he did not get his way. Over the next six years, the tantrums developed into rages. In fact, Ben broke his own television set in anger when his father refused to buy him a special video game. Ben only wanted the game because his friend had it.

I explained to Ben's father that incidents of low frustration tolerance do not usually occur in isolation. I further suggested, after spending some time with the child, that Ben was also self-centered, enjoyed feeling powerful, probably lied a lot, showed little empathy toward others, hardly ever shared his toys, and was probably stealing. Ben's father denied the stealing but reluctantly confirmed my other observations.

Though Ben did not steal or lie often, I attempted to apply the *Tough Talk* method of treatment with him. I asked Ben's father to actively take all control away from Ben by any means possible, except of course, using violence. "Once control is achieved," I told his father, "you are never to tolerate an excuse from Ben for any kind of antisocial behavior." I then explained methods of raising awareness, empathy, and guilt in Ben and discussed possible assignments to practice moral action.

Ben's father faithfully applied the method daily at home, and I saw Ben every two weeks. The results were favorable. Within a couple of months we started to see a real change in Ben. He responded especially well to the last step in the program—moral action. We had him helping other children as well as his teachers. He liked the high and sense of power he derived from engaging in moral activity and helping others.

Because of my position in several schools, I frequently discuss budding criminal children with teachers. They tell me similar stories to Ben's, about children between the ages of eight and twelve with low frustration tolerance. These stories are almost always about children who are easily distracted in class, and thus seek to create inappropriate entertainment. If they don't get what they want or their intentions are blocked, they become very angry. Teachers are forced to cope with many interruptions instigated by these young defiant children in their class.

Power and Control

Like her older counterpart, the young budding criminal from eight to twelve likes power and control and develops effective means of achieving them. One example of a power-and-control-seeking child was Rhonda, whose parents I met at a parent-teacher conference. Rhonda was eight years old, and her mother said she did not like going to bed at 9:00 P.M. Her parents told me about the problem a baby-sitter experienced one night. At bedtime their daughter carried on for two hours, crying, kicking, screaming, and arguing. Unable to calm the child down, the baby-sitter phoned the girl's grandmother for help. Unfortunately, the grandmother rushed from across town to console her granddaughter and rescue her from the baby-sitter.

As soon as the grandmother appeared, the crying stopped. Rhonda smiled knowingly, as if to say, "You see, I will get what I want and I don't want the baby-sitter here." The parents gave up and from then on seldom went out at night. They told me that their daughter simply could not get along with baby-sitters.

This is a good example of how power and control are achieved by manipulation. In many cases, the budding criminal not only manipulates adults but manipulates other children and uses them to maintain power.

This is a significant process that almost all criminal children utilize. In fact, a constant need for power and control is the second indicator that a child is developing criminal tendencies. The more a child is addicted to power, the more self-centered she becomes and the more immune she is to the effect her behavior has on others. Power is addictive, and it becomes the motivation for most criminal activity, even of children this young.

Defiant preadolescents use less sophisticated means to get control than most adult criminals, such as biting, throwing things, refusing to go to sleep, and non-stop crying. These techniques have been effective since youth, and the child has now learned to use them as manipulation devices. In addition, the child has practiced responses that she knows will generally bring her the power and control she is seeking. Thus, the cycle of manipulation and control, which began in early childhood, intensifies. In fact, young criminals in this age group, are already accomplished in their ability to control their parents and teachers. They are especially successful if they are the children of single mothers.

Those children who enjoy power eventually become grandiose, but the grandiosity, in turn, further increases the need for power. Whether the power is real or fantasy is irrelevant—in most cases, the resulting behavior is the same. The problem becomes serious if the child continues to gain power, and the power is real, allowing such a child to become very dangerous. Power based on fantasy may be less dangerous, but it is extremely pathological.

The bully between the ages of eight and twelve exemplifies the use of power and control against those who are smaller and/or weaker. By now the bullying may be crossing the line into physical abuse of other children or parents. Left untreated, bullies are prime candidates for violent criminal activity later.

The use of power and control is not restricted to one gender. However, I have found that girls generally use power differently than boys. They scheme more and are less obvious in their aggressions. They effectively use manipulation, gossip, ganging up on weaker children and the silent treatment to achieve their goals. This type of power and control is just as painful to the victim as the more overt, aggressive acts of power and control utilized by boys. It is likely that extreme victimization by powerful peers is a contributing factor in adolescent suicides and, in rare cases, homicides.

Around the ages of ten to twelve, some defiant kids start getting involved in gang activity. In general, there are two types of kids who join gangs—leaders and followers. Leaders like the power of their position and exercise considerable power over other gang members, as well as organizing them for criminal activity. The followers are looking for identification and power through the strength of the gang.

Over the last couple of years, some of the most outrageous crimes in schools and communities throughout the world have been committed by gang members. Gangs use extortion and violence, and, if well organized, they are difficult for the authorities to regulate. When gang members are so young, the law has limited power to stop them.

Resentment of Authority

By middle childhood, the young criminal's resentment of authority has increased. The defiant child has mastered what he has learned in early childhood and now utilizes different techniques to gain control. As he grows older, his oppositional behavior becomes rebellion with a cause.

This rebellious attitude is another fast way of recognizing a criminal child. One way the criminal child between the ages of eight and twelve begins to show his rebellion is in his outward appearance. For instance, he may have a visible tattoo with slogans and representations proclaiming his antisocial values, or he may wear a swastika armband. Through his appearance, the young criminal now begins to demonstrate a complete disregard for authority. Long hair is frequently unkempt; short hair may be dyed and is also unkempt. Perhaps a boy wears earrings, while both girls and boys affect gang type clothes. At the latter end of this period, boys begin to be fixated on gaining muscles and girls on looking tough in order to affect aggressive behavior.

It is almost impossible to run into a young criminal who does not have trouble with authority figures. In fact, you can probably identify such children by looking at school attendance records, the number of times sent to the principal's office, the number of fights, and so on. Though they all resent authority, when asked, many express a desire to be firemen or policemen. It is an interesting paradox that budding young criminals are attracted to such professions because of the position and power they represent rather than their responsibility for the public welfare.

Resentment of authority is easy to detect in preadolescent criminals. Many of these children initially have difficulty with their mothers and fathers and with rules and regulations of the home. When a child with deviant behavior starts school, he will find his classes boring and have problems with the teacher, vice principal, or principal. Such a child is frequently diagnosed by professionals as having a learning disability or an attention deficit (which may be true). However, if you give him something to do that he likes, he suddenly does not show any kind of learning disability or attention deficit. He is very selective in his performance. In fact, most preadolescent criminals are accomplished in shoplifting and other criminal activities that require concentration, mechanical skills, and hypervigilance.

Not long ago, I debated with a psychiatrist who had called me in to give a second opinion in the case of a twelve-year-old criminal who was an expert at stealing cars. The psychiatrist told me that he believed Attention Deficit Disorder was one of the major causes of the boy's criminal behavior, and he administered Ritalin to reduce the child's hyperactivity.

This young criminal admitted to me that he receives $500 for every car he steals and he is very successful at it. When I told him about the alleged cause of his criminality being hyperactivity, he laughed. We both agreed that: he is quite able to attend to the task of stealing; he exercises extreme concentration and watchfulness while executing the crime; he very seldom gets caught.

Excitement

Between the ages of eight and twelve, the budding criminal is always looking for excitement, and she usually finds it by getting into trouble. Just being a good kid is not exciting enough. She tries to make life into one big party.

A bully, for instance, finds it exciting to torment other children. Many criminal children begin engaging in sexual activity at an early age—this is exciting to them. Many start smoking early—this, too, is exciting. It is also more thrilling to sabotage a group activity or class than to become part of it.

Many young criminals get a real high from vandalism. Police chases are the ultimate excitement, especially if the young criminals don't get caught. Breaking rules and regulations, as well as humiliating the teacher, is exciting. Even at this young age, criminal children tell me they like to live on the edge. I often suggest substitute activities that do not involve hurting others, such as skating, hiking, camping, or fishing. Young criminals rarely engage in such activities because they find healthy activities boring. The excitement they crave is almost always against the rules and at someone else's expense. Even though they are still in grade school, many young criminals are quite adept at stealing. Hardly ever do they feel empathy for the victim of their crime or guilt for violating private property.

Recently, when I challenged Robbie, an eleven-year-old criminal, as to how unfair his crimes are, he answered, "I don't know those people. I wouldn't steal from you because I know you and I respect you."

When evaluating excitement, we need to distinguish it from mischievous behavior and insignificant vandalism or occasional stealing that many children at times may engage in. The excitement that is characteristic of the criminal child is of a much more significant degree and it is habitual. When I ask young criminals why they engage in criminal activity, almost all say they commit crimes for excitement and money (that is, after I puncture their excuses.) When a young criminal steals, he does it solely for excitement and profit. In his words, he "gets a rush" when engaging in criminal activity.

Self-Centeredness

The preadolescent criminal has developed her self-centeredness to a considerable degree. After all, she has been generally successful in her criminal behavior since the age of three or four.

Since, thus far, punishment has been an ineffective deterrent with these children, and they are quite aware that very little can be done to them (the law rarely pursues children under twelve unless they've committed a major crime), development of egocentricity is accelerated. The preadolescent criminal child usually displays an arrogant attitude and total lack of respect for adults.

On one occasion in a restaurant, I watched a mother with her eight-year-old son who showed criminal characteristics. The mother ordered a hamburger and fries for him. When the food arrived, the child started throwing fries on the floor and then screamed for ice cream. After tasting the ice cream, he also threw that on the floor, protesting it was not the flavor he wanted.

At that point, I leaned over from my table and asked the mother if she would allow me to talk to the child, explaining that I worked with difficult kids. After a brief conversation with me, her son glared at me and yelled, "I'm going to cut your f—ing head off!"

It was obvious that the child did not like me because I was aware of what he was doing. He had his mother wrapped around his little finger. Such a child only wants to be around people he can control or manipulate, and he shuns the ones he cannot.

I would like to point out that most non-criminal children slowly reduce their self-centeredness, becoming more moral and showing more pro-social behavior as they mature. However, in the case of the young criminal, the reverse is true.

As they enter their teens, young criminals become much more self-centered and less moral in their behavior. That may be why it is so hard to change the behavior of the next stage of young offenders and why so many crimes are committed by adolescents ages sixteen to eighteen.

Lying

Even at the ages of eight through twelve, the young criminal is already an accomplished liar. He lies to avoid responsibility, and he blames others for what he has done. Most of his lying is just bragging—he will describe victories in fights (sometimes real and sometimes fantasy), achievements that are not based in reality, and, at times, sexual escapades which are again mostly fantasy. Budding criminal children also lie to set people up and to make fun of them.

These children are smart enough to know how to use excuses (which is a form of lying) that are readily accepted by professionals and are also very effective in allowing young criminals to continue their conduct without being held responsible. They are also experts at playing the role of the victim.

A popular reason they give for why they commit crimes is that they were subject to child abuse when they were younger. The young criminal knows how to use this excuse to manipulate professionals' judgments about him. In fact, we should realize that, in many cases, this child abused his parents, not the other way around. In general, this excuse is usually accepted and is very effective in preventing punishment.

One of my clients, Tania, was a very gentle lady who was raising her son, Fred, by herself. At that point her son was nine and already displaying very aggressive tendencies. One day, Tania came to see me wearing dark glasses. Since I had no false illusions about her child, I immediately suspected that Fred hit her, probably because he did not get something he wanted.

Initially, the mother denied Fred hit her and said she fell and hit a table. When I pushed her further, she admitted with great embarrassment that her little darling hit her because she refused to let him watch television after 10:00 P.M. I suspect this was not the first time it happened.

I have noticed that smart young criminals are experts in telling half-lies and half-truths. For example, if a budding criminal child is at a neighbor's house and given a small thimble of beer to taste and later comes home almost drunk, she will fail to admit that she had several unauthorized beers prior to the one taste of beer she blames on the neighbor.

It has been my experience that, whether it is stealing, vandalizing, setting fires, or breaking and entering, seldom does the criminal child admit to committing a crime. She will always lie. If she is caught, she will admit the one mischief for which she got caught but never the many others she committed which go unsuspected.

Lack of Responsibility

The young criminal is a master of using excuses to avoid responsibility. The lack of responsibility occurs at home, at school, and in the community. Such a child refuses to do chores or lies about completing them. He leaves his room messy, his bed unmade, and never puts away his toys after playing with them. He makes promises and doesn't keep them. He seldom does homework.

He dislikes school because it's far too boring, and the teacher usually finds him to be the cause of a disruption in class. He will try to sabotage school projects, is irresponsible with other children, will try to get others to do a project and then pretend that he is doing his share or simply laughs at the children who are working. To him, the other kids are fools and are there to be manipulated.

One way to recognize such a child is by his total inability to take responsibility for any misdeed. Yet, he always expects a pat on the back if he does something good. He gets very annoyed if he does not get a reward for his nominal good behavior.

Distortion of Love

Like her younger and older brethren, the young criminal's concept of love is almost totally hedonistic and pleasure seeking. She seems to love only the people in her life that she can manipulate or control. If you are aware of her scheme, she will discard you and look for another person to manipulate. (Remember the baby-sitter example?) It's not an accident that many adult criminals love their grandmothers!

Such a child's concept of love is usually based on what's in it for them. A loving child is more than willing to share food and affection, whereas, the young criminal has difficulty sharing—she only takes and rarely gives anything in return. If she does give something, it is usually with an ulterior motive: you scratch my back and I'll scratch yours.

A child's ability to feel and express love usually involves learning respect, sharing, developing empathy and consideration for others, and communicating feelings. These concepts are under-developed in the young criminal. Her concept of love consists of manipulation, intimidation, being charming at times, putting her brothers and sisters down, and other ploys she designs to get what she wants. A budding criminal of eight or nine has little difficulty, especially after being caught in an outrageous act, saying to her mother or father, "I love you." In reality, in most cases this means, "Do you still love me?"

When professional therapists or school teachers meet such a child, they immediately believe the child has low self-esteem or she does not love herself. However, she loves herself so much that there is no room for others.

Lack of Awareness or Distorted Sense of Self-awareness
Self-awareness is made up of four elements: a) *knowledge* of the difference between right and wrong; b) *realization* of the impact unfair acts or behavior have on others; c) *experiencing* positive moral feelings following a good act; d) *realistic view of oneself* or self-knowledge.

The criminal child is only familiar with the element of knowledge. Seldom does he realize the impact of his actions on others or experience the positive feelings associated with doing good acts. The high that many of us experience from doing something good is seen as a ridiculous weakness from the criminal child's perspective. The budding criminal is also extremely delu-sional in regard to a realistic view of himself.

I saw this attitude when I asked Todd, an aggressive twelve-year-old criminal who was always fighting, how he would describe himself. Without any hesitation, he said, "I'm good people." I then proceeded to ask him if it was okay for good people to con-tinuously beat up other children. His answer was quite pre-dictable: "The kids I beat up deserve it. They are always in my face and treat me with disrespect."

Since self-awareness is a very popular goal employed by mental health professionals to facilitate change, I suggest that they do more harm than good with this type of child since the young criminal exhibits a very self-centered form of self-awareness.

The young criminal seldom suffers from low self-esteem. In fact, he tends to think very highly of himself, but this high self-esteem is based on distorted values. Todd, for example, bases his self-esteem on how many kids he can beat up in a week, rather than whether he can do well in school or achieve other conven-tional successes that build self-esteem in the non-criminal child.

Excuses

The eight-to-twelve-year-old budding criminal is already an expert in making excuses. He seldom, if ever, takes responsibility for his misdeeds. When lacking a good excuse, he can always ask a pro-fessional to give him one. The professional may say he's stealing for attention, he suffers from too much love or lack of it, he is abused, his father is an alcoholic, or he is influenced by wayward peers. In their book, *Excuses*, C.R. Snyder, Raymond Higgins and Rita Stucky list some of the most common excuses. They are:

1. **Denial.** "I didn't do it." This is simply refuting the charges.
2. **Creating an alibi.** "I was playing with my friend in another part of town when the break and enter occurred." This is a highly sophisticated lie beginning to be used by eleven-and-twelve-year-old criminals and used even more frequently at older ages. The young criminal may even use that alibi if

she left a piece of her clothing or her fingerprints at the scene of the crime.

3. **Blaming.** "The dog ate the pie." "My sister stole the money." As you will see later, therapists frequently give children and young adults an opportunity to blame society, poverty, bad parents, etc.

4. **Minimizing.** "I only hit him a couple of times. What's the big deal? He was only bleeding from his nose." The budding criminals who commit breaking and enterings will have lots of money and so can afford to pay up once in awhile when they are caught.

5. **Justification.** Recently, eleven-year-old Jake told me that his father asked him to steal for him. I asked for his father's telephone number and was "playing poker" with the boy by pretending that I knew his father. When I pressed him with that point, he admitted that 80 percent of the time he stole because he liked it and without his father's knowledge. I believe he stole closer to 100 percent of the time without the encouragement of his father.

6. **Derogation.** "I hit my sister because she's bad and deserves it!" "This boy is a sissy and likely a faggot and that's a good reason to beat him up!" Sometimes, the young criminal will tell me that for excitement he will go looking for a "faggot" to beat up in a park or some hidden place.

Manipulation
Even non-criminal children try their hands at manipulation as they reach the preteens.

At the age of twelve, my daughter was supposed to visit my wife and me in a different city from where she lived with her mother. My wife and I had already made arrangements to go on a vacation, and we asked my daughter if she wanted to join us. Very excited, she said yes, and we went to great expense and trouble to get another vacation package for her. When she arrived, I noticed that she was spending considerable time on the phone talking to her boyfriend. At the end of the conversation, she telephoned her mother, crying her eyes out and telling her mother she wanted to go home. Her mother immediately arranged for my daughter to return home.

I believe this is a very good example of how a young girl, who likely wanted to see her boyfriend, was able to take advantage of the disharmony and lack of communication between father and mother to achieve her end. We sent her home but were liable for the additional expense of the vacation package.

In comparison to the previous example, manipulative behavior in criminal children is much more exaggerated and is the rule rather than the exception. Temper tantrums and rages are very effective means of getting what is wanted. They often try to play one parent against the other and frequently exploit unwitting grandparents. They are experts in taking advantage of disharmony among the adult authority figures, both at home and at school.

Lack of Empathy

Even at eight to twelve years old, the criminal child is totally oblivious to the feelings of others, particularly those who are most affected by his behavior. His self-centeredness has blocked the development of empathy. Rather, all his energy is used to look after number one, leaving no energy left to care about others.

In fact, developing a lack of empathy is a gradually accelerating process. The more time the budding young criminal spends looking after number one, the more self-centered he becomes and the less capable he is of feeling for others.

As I've indicated, I strongly believe that empathy is one of the main ingredients of morality. Yet, some parents, as well as our education system, fail to teach children how to develop empathy. In the case of potentially criminal children, the educational effort needs to be many times more intense if we wish to diminish the number of criminals in society.

The role of empathy will be discussed in greater detail in a separate chapter.

Impulsiveness

At ages eight through twelve, the young criminal is very impulsive. She habitually acts before she thinks.

Almost all aggressive behavior is an expression of impulsiveness. One should not confuse impulsiveness with spontaneity. Spontaneity is usually viewed as a mark of creativity, while impulsiveness is a trait common to self-centered, pleasure-seeking children.

For example, many impulsive young criminals have increasing difficulty in middle school, not because they have learning disabilities as some professionals claim, but because they are too impulsive to focus long enough on any task that doesn't excite them.

They are seldom satisfied with one activity and jump from one thing to another, frequently destroying toys and furniture at home, and books and equipment at school. You can certainly spot them in department stores where they abuse products and displays. Unfortunately, you rarely see anyone trying to stop them, especially not the parents.

Impulsive criminal children are opportunists. Whatever appears to be an easy pushover activity or person becomes their target. They generally act before they think, also an example of impulsive tendencies.

Just recently, Nicole, a friend of mine, had her car stolen four times from the same parking spot. Each time, the car was returned with minor damage. When Nicole told me the story, I stated that I had no doubt kids were stealing her car, and they soon would be caught because now the police knew they were stealing on a regular basis. Sure enough, a week later, the young criminals were caught speeding in Nicole's car. Later, I shared this story with some young teenage offenders. They laughed and asked what kind of criminals these were who acted without stopping to think that the police would get wise to them. Sure enough, the youngsters who stole the car were only twelve years old. They are young criminals, yet they have not developed the sophistication of the next stage of criminality (the teenager).

Treatment Application

I have used the *Tough Talk* method, which I've mentioned and which will be discussed in more detail later, many times with individual children from eight to twelve. I have had some successes and some failures. Following, is an example of success and also one of failure.

First, the success story. One of my clients, Mona Cummings, who is a police officer, was raising her son, Billy, alone. She came to me totally frustrated by her child's behavior and the fact that he was being administered drugs to counteract his conduct. Billy was nine years old, extremely hyperactive and quite violent. He was physically bigger than other nine-year-old boys, and he intimidated his classmates to the extent where he was suspended from school for beating them up.

When I interviewed Mona, I was immediately comforted by the fact that she was open-minded enough to see the benefits of my method. Also, because of her own experiences with criminals, Mona felt the method had a good chance for success with her boy, whereas the drugs already prescribed (a tranquilizer and Ritalin) reduced his hyperactivity but did not stop the violent and generally oppositional behavior.

I tested Billy's intelligence and also assessed his behavior, using the list I've compiled of characteristics of the young criminal. He seemed to fit most of them, scoring high on self-centeredness, resentment of authority, low frustration tolerance, and strong desires for power and control. However, I was also pleasantly surprised to find that he did show compassion and empathy toward his mother and rather quickly toward me as I started to see him regularly. I felt that we were dealing with a good candidate for successful application of the *Tough Talk* method.

I asked Mona to arrange a meeting with Billy's teacher and the school principal so that they would understand the method and we would have complete cooperation at the school. As the boy already showed the capacity for empathy, it was not too difficult to show him that his mother, his teacher, and I were distressed when he was violent towards other children.

Billy's self-awareness of his actions was also enhanced by systematically teaching him to replace hurting behavior with helping behavior. I also asked his teacher to pick out a child in school who was usually treated badly by others. "I want you to ask Billy to assist him and act as his bodyguard," I instructed her, recalling my own experience when my father used a similar character-building technique with me many years ago. The results were remarkable! Billy not only changed, but even his academic progress, which had suffered previously, improved dramatically.

A follow-up of Billy over the last three years suggests that he is still doing very well. There has been only one incident of violence at school since we applied the *Tough Talk* method.

Unfortunately, not all my cases turn out as well as Billy's. Twelve-year-old Joey was referred to me by a pediatrician because he was failing in school. This was especially significant in his case because an intelligence test done by the school showed Joey to be extremely intelligent. When I interviewed Joey's parents and the school authorities, I also found out that he engaged in constant fighting and vandalism. Since Joey was an only child, I suspected that he was somewhat spoiled. The most common scenario in situations like this is that the father is tough and restrictive while the mother tends to spoil the child. However, in this case the opposite was true, and his parents constantly argued in front of him as to the best way to discipline him.

I attempted to convince Joey's parents that the only way we could achieve any kind of change in Joey's behavior was for them to present a united front. I also introduced them to the *Tough Talk* method. Initially, Joey responded well because I was able to establish a relationship with him, often challenging him to games of chess and checkers. Yet, a month later, the report from his school suggested that very little change in his disruptive behavior had occurred.

My investigation at the school indicated the authorities there were cooperating with my method. The only other possible problem area was, I felt, the home. I invited Joey's parents for interviews and realized that there was considerable tension between them. The mother was the stronger personality in the home. The father was passive/aggressive and, because the parents had an unhappy union, the father was using Joey, consciously or unconsciously, to sabotage my method. My attempt to patch up the relationship between the parents failed. In fact, three months later the parents were discussing a trial separation.

I have found in my years of experience with budding criminal children that, though authorities frequently blame the home life, this is not usually the major reason for a child to exhibit criminal behavior. However, I do believe the reason that Joey did not demonstrate a significant change could, in his case, be blamed on the disharmony at home. To increase the possibility of success in such situations, you need cooperation from all adults involved directly or indirectly with the child. Parents may have to put aside marital differences for the moment in order to present a unified front so their child can be helped.

If we get cooperation from school, home and other professionals involved in a difficult case, good results may be achieved. Without it, failure is quite predictable.

9

A Day in the Life of a Budding Criminal, Sixteen-Year-Old George

George is a sixteen-year-old juvenile offender who will likely spend the rest of his life in and out of jail. Using jail jargon, he is doing life on the installment plan.

George lives on the street because his parents could not cope with him, and in fact, his father is an abuser. His parents failed him, and in my opinion, the system also failed him because it perceives him as a victim, rather than a victimizer. George supports himself by stealing and selling drugs. His criminal activities usually alternate between dealing drugs, breaking and entering, and, occasionally, stealing cars. From the point of view of his subculture values, he is quite successful. George has already spent two or three years in juvenile facilities.

He told me the following story when we met for a pre-trial conference.

Around eleven o'clock one Saturday night, George went to a party with friends (some of his friends are nineteen- or twenty-year-old criminals). The party lasted until five in the morning. It started as usual with heavy drinking, smoking marijuana, and occasionally using other drugs like cocaine or heroin. George prefers to smoke marijuana but has experimented with cocaine, which gives him a great high. He told me, "It's better than sex!" George denies that he is addicted to alcohol, drugs, or sex. In his own defense, he explains, "I sell drugs but I'm too smart to use too much myself."

A few hours into the party, George tried to force himself on a young girl who was ignoring him. Somehow he managed to tear her dress before two other males stopped him. The girl did not call the police because she didn't want to be referred to as a rat. She was lucky this time that she was not sexually assaulted. At five in the morning, the party ended and George and a friend went to sleep in a condemned house in the downtown area, where he slept until two in the afternoon.

George's main fantasy is a big score. He recently started casing a house nearby with only one person living in it. The man usually left the house in the morning and didn't return until late at night. George's only concern was that there was a German shepherd dog in the backyard of the house. In order to break in, he would have to do something about the dog. George had already found out which poison he could put on a piece of meat in order to kill the dog quickly. That day he planned to do it.

Around six o'clock in the evening near dusk, George went to the house with the poisoned piece of meat and threw it to the dog. The shepherd immediately ate the meat and died within a half-hour. George jumped over the fence, broke a window and climbed into the house looking for cash and jewelry.

George had experience breaking into houses and small businesses and knew how to disconnect the alarm system once he was inside. However, he was unaware of the silent alarm system in the bedroom where there was a safe containing money and valuable jewelry. George was mainly interested in these items because they were light and easy to carry if he had to run quickly.

While George was busy looking for the cash and jewelry and a possible safe if he could find one, the alarm was already alerting police at the nearby station. The police arrived while George was still in the bedroom and caught him in the act. This time, George may receive a longer sentence.

DIFFERENT CATEGORIES WITHIN THE JUVENILE CRIMINAL'S SUBCULTURE

Based on my experience, juvenile offenders are of three categories:

A) Roughly 10 to 20 percent of juvenile offenders respond to the cognitive moral approach. This group shows good capacity for feeling empathy, remorse and guilt.

B) Approximately 50 percent have the capacity for empathy but our present methods of stimulating these feelings are ineffective.

C) About 30 percent, I believe, are hopeless and, like George, will spend the rest of their lives in jail. We have an obligation to try to help these offenders, but I am very pessimistic about the outcome.

What Can Be Done

I believe that juvenile offenders in categories A and B can be reached using the cognitive moral approach. To get good results, an adult counselor must first build a relationship with the juvenile, progress toward teaching discipline and moral values, and then to inculcating a responsible lifestyle. This is best done using one-on-one rather than group therapy.

If a counselor is unsuccessful in treating the B category offender, this may be attributed to two major factors:

1) Lack of understanding by the counselor of the depths of the criminality and self-centeredness;

2) Failure of professionals to acknowledge that the main problem is in the juvenile himself, rather than in his environment. There is no question that there is a high correlation between abuse, neglect, poverty, and criminality. However, changing those conditions is much more difficult than changing the juvenile himself.

I am saddened that so many professionals are still providing excuses and holding on to psychological/psychiatric methods that, in many cases, promote criminality rather than reduce it. Again, if we view criminality as extreme self-centeredness, all treatment should be aimed at reducing self-centeredness.

I believe that a majority of the boot camp methods fail to produce desired results because they emphasize discipline without also establishing proper values. If we provide a juvenile offender with discipline without teaching values, we have a disciplined criminal who is even more dangerous. I believe boot camp would be considerably more beneficial if it were combined with my cognitive moral method.

I recently visited an institution that is trying very hard to break the criminal subculture. Even swearing is discouraged and punished. There is great attention provided to keep the juvenile offender busy, and the institution seems to have created a milieu where all the staff (professionals, correctional officers, kitchen workers) practice and believe in the method they use. I was very impressed because they have orchestrated treatment in a way that does not allow the juvenile offender to manipulate the system for his benefit as usually occurs in other institutions.

Today's increase in violence by juvenile criminals is very frightening, especially by juveniles who commit outrageous crimes and murders. One juvenile with whom I recently talked was involved in a ghastly murder. He claimed that he did it because he lost his girlfriend; however, the real reason was that he is addicted to power. To him, losing his girlfriend meant he lost his power over her, and the use of a gun was an expression of his unwillingness to relinquish power.

Violence in groups, especially gangs, has more momentum, and there is considerable research on this subject. Since it takes a certain amount of courage to commit murder, gang and peer support provides the extra reinforcement for such acts. Although much juvenile crime comes from the gang culture, youth crime today knows no class, religion, or ethnic group.

Not long ago, I worked intensely with Ted, a teenage juvenile who had killed a member of the local community for what appeared to be an unjustifiable reason. Ted came from a middle-class good home and caring family. One wonders why someone like him would kill. What I found surprising about him was that he was a leader in my group, highly intelligent, friendly and quite likable. After getting to know him, I concluded that the killing was an expression of a power surge brought on by a friend with similar tendencies. When I asked Ted why he did it, he admitted that he simply wanted to know what it felt like to kill someone.

There is no rational explanation for the killing if we look for a reason in his environment. Ted killed because he liked it. It has been my experience that many juveniles commit crimes because they like what they are doing. In my groups, every week I ask young boys and girls who are juvenile offenders why they committed their crimes. Almost always the answers are the same—we like it! It's exciting! The money, the rush, the power!

In discussing possible ways of dealing with juvenile offenders, we should clearly understand what we are dealing with and that there are different classifications within the subculture. Some young criminals will respond well to my approach, others will not.

The first task is to assess them properly. The system generally tends to assess offenders by the number of their crimes or the severity of a particular crime. This may be quite misleading. I have seen adult criminals who committed murders, but have more moral attributes than other criminals who merely shoplift or drink and drive. Since it is my belief that one's moral fiber will decide whether a person will change or not, obviously the assessment should be based on that. We need to ask ourselves:

1. What is the degree and extent of criminality? This can be assessed by first studying the criminal offenders' histories from police records and interviews with the family, relatives, teachers, and police. Also, we should use the thirteen characteristics I've enumerated and, if at all possible, have two or three independent observers assess the offenders, using the characteristics as a model.

For example, let's examine the characteristic of *Resentment of Authority*. Ask a teacher who has taught the young offender how he would rate Johnny from zero to ten, using the *Resentment of Authority* category and the *Lying* category. A professional who is also familiar with the thirteen characteristics should be able to rate the young offender after an extensive interview by asking questions that relate to the characteristics.

2. Assess what capacity the juvenile offender has to appreciate and practice responsible and moral behavior. This can be done if we get some idea of his or her ability to feel empathy, remorse, and guilt. The motivation for change is directly related to this last point; the more capacity for empathy, remorse and guilt, the more the person can be motivated to change. A counselor experienced with young offenders should have a good sense of the questions to ask.

Besides the traditional method of tracing an individual's criminal history from police records or discussing his history with relatives and the offender himself, we should also ask him the following questions.

1. Is there anybody you really care for?
2. Do you realize that you are hurting the people you love?
3. Did you ever feel badly for hurting them or do you feel badly now?
4. Do you wish to continue hurting them and why do they deserve it?
5. Do you consider yourself a good person?
6. Does a good person go on hurting the people he loves?

My experience suggests that if the juvenile is connected to somebody (a mother, child, brother, or committed girlfriend), there is a better chance that some of the responses to the questions will be affirmative. Many juvenile offenders, when asked these questions, respond to them with hostility or sarcasm. Even if they answer in the affirmative, one senses that there is no sincerity behind their answers.

In some cases one can test the validity of the answers by talking with a relative. I generally ask if it is all right for me to call the relative. Jake, whom I briefly described earlier, blamed his father for his crimes. When I pushed him for his father's telephone number, Jake admitted that 80 percent of his crimes were done without his father's knowledge.

If we categorize young criminals according to their abilities to practice moral behavior, it is then a question of deciding which method is the best to use with them.

Category C, the last and most difficult 30 percent, will only respond (if at all) to what psychologists call behavior modification or reinforcement therapy.

To a large extent the best method to use in treating a juvenile offender depends on the setting we are talking about—a jail, open custody, institution, group home, or simply a school or regular home. Each method has to be applied differently, depending on the facility.

If the criminal behavior shows in the school *and* we get cooperation from the school and parents *and* if the offender is judged to be in category A or B, then there is a better chance for success. In an open custody setting, we have improved odds because the juvenile is connected to the community and there are ways of reinforcing pro-social behavior and checking if indeed she is practicing what she is being taught. The most difficult setting is, of course, a jail. In jail, a juvenile offender is subject to strong subculture pressure that reinforces criminality. Seldom is there agreement among the professionals as to which method is the best to use. A psychologist may believe in behavioral modification while a psychiatrist may prefer to administer drugs. Those two treatment methods may conflict with each other, especially when applied to juveniles. This is a subject I will discuss later.

The attributes of the people dealing with juvenile delinquents greatly influence the results achieved. A counselor cannot teach responsibility unless he or she is a responsible person. A counselor cannot teach morality unless the counselor is moral. A counselor cannot teach empathy unless he or she consistently shows sensitivity to others. A counselor cannot teach respect unless the counselor is respectful. Some employees of the correctional system truly believe that the only way to deal with offenders is to lock them up and throw the key away.

Such an attitude will certainly be picked up by the juveniles themselves. This will give them an excuse and reason to resent the system, viewing it as hostile and unfriendly. It can provide them with sufficient excuses to continue doing what they are doing. We must talk to offenders (or anybody else for that matter) with respect and without prejudice. Anyone who is not willing to do so has no business trying to help the young delinquent. After all, we do call jails correctional centers; their intended purpose is to rehabilitate.

10

Juvenile Offenders (Children Between 13 and 17 Years)

Scenario #1: Two thirteen-year-olds are out on bail after being charged with savagely beating a nine-year-old boy. The nine-year-old was attacked, and when his baby-sitter tried to help, she was thrown to the ground and kicked. They have also caused $60,000 worth of vandalism in a local school.

Scenario #2: A fourteen-year-old thief viciously assaults a seventy-five-year-old woman. The woman suffers a broken nose, a badly sprained arm, and bruised ribs. The teenager was trying to steal her purse.

Scenario #3: A pregnant thirteen-year-old murders a telephone repairman. She just walks up to the victim and shoots him in the head. Prosecutors describe her as a killer with "nerves of steel."

As we approach the millennium, the whole issue of criminality in juveniles must be viewed in light of escalating juvenile violence in the last few years. The incidents of children robbing, killing and molesting other children and torturing animals is increasing, and the public has become frightened of these young criminal children. In the United States, many violent juveniles are being prosecuted as adults. Other countries are also grappling with child crime. Should we blame the system? Should we blame the parents? What is happening? I would like to provide some explanations I have formulated through my research and long experience with juvenile offenders.

Dr. Stanton Samenow said in his book, *Inside the Criminal Mind*, that all traditional explanations for criminality such as poverty, neglect, abuse, drugs, and alcohol, may be half-truths which do not tell the whole story. I agree. Budding criminal children seem to have exaggerated amounts of self-centeredness right from birth. Recognizing that adolescents are generally self-centered as part of their human development, we understand how the self-centeredness of juvenile offenders can thus be considerably greater than that of non-criminal teenagers.

Furthermore, the subculture inhabited by many juvenile offenders reinforces criminality and sometimes kills the capacity to feel for others. A young criminal who does not feel empathy and has a distorted concept of respect is frequently drunk on power, receives support in his quest for power from his peers and the subculture, and is at times quite dangerous.

There are important similarities and differences between juvenile and adult criminality.

SIMILARITIES

Power and Control.

It has been my experience that, like adult criminals, the majority of juvenile delinquents are intoxicated by power and control. This heightened sense of domination blocks awareness of human compassion and love. As discussed previously, young criminals are experts in maintaining power and control and they are supported by different sources, who are at a loss to know what to do with them, such as parents, indulgent or fearful grandparents, lawyers and professionals. This point will be discussed later.

By the time these experts in gaining control go to jail, their family and teachers have almost given up trying to change them. Remember that many juvenile offenders are experienced criminals. A boy of seventeen, who has been involved with crime since the age of five, already has twelve years of delinquent experience. We should not be fooled by his young age. He is very familiar with the criminal subculture and is knowledgeable about juvenile law and legal loopholes to benefit his cause.

Peer pressure and gang activity are extremely important in gaining power and control. When a young criminal joins a gang, he is much more dangerous because he now has the power of the group behind him. Furthermore, stories of gang violence in the media show that these groups do in fact wield a dangerous power.

Resentment of Authority.

The attitudes of most juvenile offenders are extremely oppositional. The way they sit, carry themselves and walk, and their body language clearly suggests they are unmindful of the people around them, especially if someone in authority tries to tell them what to do.

Their idea of freedom is, *to hell with everyone else—I am the boss!* They resent adults such as teachers, school principals, police, and at times, a strict father or mother who tries to put limits on their deviant behavior. Rather than seeing juvenile delinquents as victims of authority figures, I have seen that in many cases they are the victimizers.

For several years Davey Young, an ex-con who graduated from my *Tough Talk* program, and occasionally myself, served as consultants to a support group of parents with explosive children. Frequently in that group, the parents discussed how much they were victimized by their adolescent children. In many of the situations, the kids were not only verbally antagonistic but physically abusive towards their parents, especially if the parent was a single mother. Many parents were afraid for their lives, and this is one reason why a lot of parent-victims do not report violence by adolescent children to the police.

Excitement.

Jason, a juvenile offender, recently asked me when I had last been to a party. I told him I had recently gone to a friend's Thanksgiving party. Jason then asked what we did there, and I told him we talked, had a couple of drinks, and ate. I had to be at work the next morning and left early. Jason thought that was very funny and laughed at me. His idea of excitement was to start partying around midnight and finish at six in the morning. By that time, drugs and alcohol would have taken their effect, and the participants would have achieved an exciting high. Sex would be a bonus. Jason was an expert at stealing cars. He told me that the high he got from a police chase was equivalent to a sexual high and he just loved it.

Many problem juveniles look at life very similarly to many adult criminals—it's all one big party. If their fun is at someone else's expense, so be it. In fact, they are experts in providing excuses for the crimes they commit and frequently blame the victim—if you leave your keys in the car, you deserve what you get! If you leave jewelry in the house, you are stupid enough to lose it!

Lying.

The juvenile offender is an accomplished liar and is smart enough to mix a little bit of truth in with the lies. She tends to lie so much that even she believes what she says. Most of her lies serve to either avoid responsibility so that she does not get into trouble or brag to boost her self-esteem.

I recently asked Carolyn, an attractive, well-dressed young woman with blonde hair and saucer-like eyes, what was the largest amount she ever had in her pocket. She said $17,000. Gaining or imagining gaining huge amounts of money by deviant methods whets the appetites of delinquents like Carolyn who believe that only idiots work for a living.

People who are not familiar with innocent looking liars like Carolyn can easily be fooled by them. Just ask any policeman or experienced counselor, and she or he will tell you how much young criminals lie, regardless of their babyish looks.

Lying can be divided into two categories—deliberate and pathological. A deliberate liar needs a good memory and consistency in his or her stories, and it has been my experience that most juvenile offenders neither have good memories nor consistency in lying.

Pathological liars are more difficult to detect than deliberate liars because they believe in their lies. Typical lies of the pathological type are what psychologists generally define as projection. When a juvenile offender explains his violent actions by saying, "I beat up this guy at a party because I didn't like the way he looked at my girlfriend," he is projecting his own anger onto an innocent victim. After all, he also had the option to take it as a compliment that someone was looking at his girlfriend.

Some juvenile offenders truly believe that their problems are primarily drinking and drugs rather than criminality. They often say that if they did not drink, they would not be violent or that they only steal to support their drug habit. If you repeat such a lie long enough, you will believe it. Psychologists call it rationalization. The truth is that drinking only gives the juvenile courage to do what he or she wants to do anyway, and using drugs is another symptom of their hedonistic pleasure-seeking self-centeredness. Juvenile offenders do not take drugs because they have an addiction; they take drugs because they like it. It is another symptom of their self-centeredness. In later chapters I will show that the word "addiction" is used far too widely and loosely. I believe it is nothing more in most cases than a sophisticated excuse or pathological lie.

Manipulation.

Like many adult criminals, juvenile delinquents are experts at manipulation. They manipulate their parents, teachers, social workers, lawyers, and the system in general.

Peter, a fourteen-year-old adolescent I was called in to examine, systematically stole at school. When the principal brought this to my attention, I immediately attempted to take control away from

Peter. Then, I attempted to show Peter how he was affecting others by teaching him the concepts of respect and empathy so that he would take responsibility for his own deeds.

My attempts completely failed because Peter managed to gain the support and allegiance of a teacher who liked him. Peter manipulated her and convinced her that his behavior was a product of a bad family situation. His brother and father were in jail, and his father was also an alcoholic. However, Peter neglected to mention that he also had a fifteen-year-old sister in the same school who came from the same environment and who was a model child.

I never tried to verify his other stories; however, there is still no excuse for his stealing. Once his manipulation of the teacher was effective, he began regaining the power he had yielded to me and became very aggressive towards me. One day he strode over to me and threatened, "You're going down." I took his warning very seriously.

Such a scenario is not uncommon in school systems. A dedicated and intelligent professional counselor begins to get results but is ultimately unsuccessful because the adolescent child cleverly manipulates another teacher or administrator to regain the power he temporarily lost.

Excuses.

Both adult offenders and juvenile delinquents are experts at excuses. Seldom do they take responsibility for their crimes. The trouble they get into is always someone else's fault. One of the best excuses I heard recently was that of a fifteen-year-old offender who told me the reason he was doing crime was because his mother was a lesbian. He also stated that a psychiatrist had put the idea into his head. Such excuses should not be acknowledged and are, of course, nonsense.

In his book, *Killer Kids*, Peter Reinhart lists fifty excuses that are used by juvenile offenders and society to explain crime. Some of the more common ones are living in poverty, alcohol abuse, physical abuse, falling victim to an unfair school system, living in a foster home, having the wrong friends, having parents who are criminals, being bad seeds, and having a learning disability like ADD (a favorite used by psychiatrists because they can then prescribe Ritalin), etc.

DIFFERENCES

Lack of Mask.

Generally, adult criminals are more sophisticated and frequently wear masks that disguise their intentions and criminality. Many smart criminals are very charming and friendly and one has to spend some time with these characters to realize that they are still criminals. Sometimes it is too late—they may already have success-fully manipulated you.

Although some do, many juvenile criminals, with the exception of grandiose children who turn to crime, do not exhibit masking and they are easier to detect. Their attitude reflects their criminality. They have chips on their shoulders and bad manners.

In teaching responsibility to juvenile offenders, I continu-ously struggle with adolescents over the way they eat. They throw food, they dirty the cafeteria, and they may steal food from each other. Dr. Prem Gupta, one of my colleagues, told me of one expe-rience he had when giving a talk to a large group of juvenile offenders who ranged in age from sixteen to seventeen. He noticed one of them picking up a big pot of coffee and carrying it back to his table. Dr. Gupta thought this was a polite kid who was going to pour coffee for everyone. The kid proceeded to drink the three liters of coffee himself!

Lack of Empathy.

Despite their bad manners and surly attitudes, most juvenile delin-quents are capable of feeling empathy for the people they love and even for their victims at times. However, it is much more difficult to arouse feelings of empathy in adolescent criminals than in non-criminal youths. Juveniles are more into power and are very self-centered. The criminal lifestyle of the juvenile delinquent tends to block the capacity for empathy and compassion. Alcohol, drugs, sex, and a lot of partying make it easy to block moral feelings.

There is another reason why it is very difficult to arouse empathy in defiant teenagers. It has been my experience that these juveniles took their apprenticeship in crime at home—that is where their self-centeredness started. They practiced by stealing money from their mothers' purses. Since many of the homes are fatherless, it is easier for such problem adolescents to maintain criminal lifestyles and alienate themselves from the people closest to them, especially their siblings and mothers.

Since empathy is easier to arouse in people who feel love and juvenile delinquents act as though they love nobody, it is quite a task to stimulate their moral qualities.

Dennis and Frank are two teenagers whom I met with several years ago at a local jail. I was amazed by the similarities of their offenses and family backgrounds. Both came from dysfunctional families. Both admitted to doing mostly car thefts and break and enters for three or four years before they were caught. As suggested by my earlier discussion of risk factors in young children, they had both been in trouble since the very early ages of three and four.

Dennis and Frank were part of a cognitive moral group I conducted which I based on an article I published called "Changing the Criminal." The article emphasized not only intellectual understanding of the criminal mind and personality, but also the understanding of emotional aspects such as empathy, respect, consideration and compassion for others.

Though at first I noted Dennis and Frank's similarities, as time went on, differences between them started to become obvious. While Frank showed considerable remorse, empathy and respect towards his family members, Dennis did not show any of these traits. I made a note to myself that the risk of Frank becoming a repeat offender was significantly less than that of Dennis.

In fact, this turned out to be an accurate prediction. It did not take long for Dennis to appear in the adult justice system. In the last five years, I have seen him in and out of jail numerous times, and each crime he is convicted of is more serious than the last. During one of his incarcerations, Dennis became a member of another group of mine in the adult section of the jail where we were discussing the fact that some criminals break into homes during Christmas and steal presents meant for young children. Dennis said he has done this himself and did not see anything wrong with it. "I think it is quite funny," he laughed. Two or three other members of the group were so angry at his attitude that I had a difficult time preventing them from beating him up. Not surprisingly, he did not return to future group meetings.

Frank, however, has appeared in jail as an adult only once in the last five years. He was very embarrassed for me to see him there and willingly admitted that he had committed a drinking and driving offense.

These two young men demonstrate that when you notice evidence of empathy and compassion towards the family by a juvenile offender, it can serve as a good predictor for reduction in crime and perhaps even elimination of it. However, when you do not see the evidence of empathy and compassion, it is likely you will see the juvenile offender serving time down the road in an adult facility.

Dennis and Frank are typical of criminals I have seen in correction facilities over the past two decades. Again, and I will repeat this important concept in many ways throughout the book, it is not enough for the delinquent to understand right from wrong or to understand criminal thinking to make him change. Only if you can tap into his emotions can you begin to see significant changes.

Attitude.

Though there are many similarities, the most significant difference between adult and juvenile delinquents is their general attitude towards authority figures and towards each other. While adult criminals are generally respectful and at times, even very charming to the authorities, the juvenile is not. Juveniles show lack of respect towards authority as well as in the way they carry themselves, the way they sit and their eating habits.

Over the past ten years working with juveniles in a group setting, in order to instill responsible behavior, I have continuously reminded them to remove their feet from the tables or another chair and not to throw leftover food on the floor. It has been my experience that if I don't use the same subculture language they do in trying to correct their behavior, they will not relate to me in a meaningful way.

In all my years of doing group work with juvenile delinquents, I have never seen one genuine example of sharing and giving during my early work with them. Their initial attitude has always been *take, take, take* and *give me, give me, give me!* In fact, when a juvenile offender does share anything, it is usually a form of bragging after a successful burglary.

The statistical breakdown of crimes committed by juveniles is generally 70 percent break and enters or stealing cars, 20 percent violent assaults and 10 percent sexual offenses. Police often say it is a lot easier to catch a juvenile offender for two reasons: 1) juveniles seem to consistently rat on each other, without ever admitting it, and 2) they are very careless about leaving evidence—fingerprints, personal belongings, etc. This probably reflects their immaturity. In other words, they may be criminals but they are not good at their trade.

There are differences in effective treatment methods, too. While experienced adult criminals frequently respond very well to the group process, most juvenile offenders are too busy trying to impress their peers in the jail setting. The strong subculture pressure reduces the effectiveness of group work with juveniles. However, when I deal with juveniles on an individual basis, I find that many do show the capacity for feeling and empathy towards the people they love but seldom, if ever, towards the victim.

Lifestyle Differences.
While some adult criminals are very much involved in an unwholesome lifestyle including alcohol, drugs, sex, violence, power, and of course greed, not all of them are necessarily involved in that

lifestyle. Such a lifestyle is more common among lower class criminals than criminals from the middle class.

With regards to juvenile offenders, a lifestyle featuring alcohol, drugs and violence is almost universal. Teenage criminals are all involved in drugs and alcohol, with an incredible amount of time spent partying. When Randall Smith and Elliot Noma examined the delinquent careers of 767 adolescents, they found that the majority were chronic offenders with an average of 11.7 arrests each. Most of them committed crimes against property that eventually developed into serious violence against people. Quite a few also stole automobiles. Just about all of them abused drugs and alcohol.

My experience with thousands of juvenile offenders over the last ten years is similar. I have seldom run into one who was not involved in breaking and enterings, stealing cars, and abusing drugs or alcohol. Just about all of them smoked marijuana. Many of them were promiscuous—although, of course, some were just bragging.

Taking into consideration the usual hedonistic pleasure-seeking behavior of juvenile offenders, it is not surprising that their lifestyle is usually connected to the use of drugs, alcohol and sex.

When examining the criminal record of 24,398 middle-aged inmates, Langon and Greenfield noticed that almost all of them had started their careers between the ages of seven and seventeen. I would suggest again that "seven" is not representative of today's budding criminals.

When I interview typical young criminals, (and I interview many of them), the story is almost always the same. He will say he started his criminal career at the age of twelve. I discount this. Why does he say age twelve? That's when the juvenile offender started to be noticed by the police. Prior to that age, the authorities were not usually involved. When I probe deeper and ask them, the teens usually laugh, admitting that their careers indeed began at a much earlier age, usually three or four. I have seen very few juvenile offenders who do not fit the picture I have described. No wonder a high percentage of them progress to adult jails.

Knowledge of early development of criminal activities and risk factors is extremely important. If we hope to prevent criminality, we need to realize that at the age of twelve, the juvenile criminal has seven or eight years of experience in the criminal lifestyle. The system has failed to realize the seriousness of the problem or has given up trying to change the behavior long before the child becomes a juvenile offender who reaches the courts.

11

How Parents and the System Contribute to Criminality in Children

"Is it the parents fault that kids become criminals?" This is a common question. Traditional thinking generally blames a young criminal's parents by focusing on the incidences of neglect, abuse, single parenting, alcoholism, and poverty as the reason for criminal behavior. There is no question there is high correlation between these factors and criminality, but to suggest that parents cause criminality is questionable.

My experience with juvenile offenders leads me to believe there is no easy answer. For example, if we accept the proposition that parents produce criminals, how do we explain a family with four children, three of whom do well in school and are socially responsible, while only one exhibits all the characteristics of a budding criminal? By the same token, how do we explain the children who come from the worst environments and yet become highly responsible people?

Tedious searches for answers will only provide criminal juveniles with further excuses for their criminality. It is my contention that young offenders make a choice very early in life to go their own way and do their own thing. For many of them, no amount of discipline, education or effort by parents, schools, or professionals will prevent the development of criminality. Instead of spending a lot of time and energy seeking causes, I have found it much more beneficial to characterize criminality and identify it in the budding criminal at a *very* early age. Then we have a good opportunity to change the bad behavior and begin to teach responsible behavior. However, it has been my experience that some parents (sometimes through no fault of their own) do considerable damage and contribute to their child's criminality. The following are some of the things that parents do wrong.

1) Parents often give the budding criminal too much control very early in life. Since the budding criminal is an expert in getting control from a very early age, he knows how to get it either through temper tantrums, manipulation, or lying. Parents trying to accommodate the child by giving him what he wants essentially allow the child to maintain control. If you continue to give a child control very early in life, attempts to change his behavior later become more difficult.

Education manuals and self-help books that recommend parents not get into a control battle with their child are, in my experience, mistaken. You must stay in control of a child at any cost or you may see the budding criminal develop into an accomplished liar, thief, or violent offender.

2) Since the parent is not aware that the budding criminal is extremely self-centered—more so than non-criminal children—the parent tends to make comments about how cute he is or how spirited he is, all in the name of creating a self-confidant and independent child. However, the parent is only feeding the criminal child's destructive self-centeredness.

3) Many parents make the mistake of teaching their children that the world outside is unfair and untrustworthy. I recall an anecdote once told to me: a boy went to the second floor of a building, and his father on the ground told him to jump, holding out his hands in readiness. The boy jumped and broke a leg

because his father was unable to catch him. The message to a child is very clear—you can't even trust your father. This is an example of what I call "gangster mentality"—you can't trust anyone—and surely contributes to child criminality.

4) Often parents take a child's side in a school disciplinary matter rather than support the teacher or principal involved because they feel no one else understands how brilliant their child is. Teaching a child not to obey authority is a sure way of providing the child with more weapons to manipulate the school and other authorities. In addition, if the parents fight with one another, the child can pursue the game at everyone's expense.

5) When parents disagree about a discipline problem, one parent takes the child's side. Siding with the child is a sure way of contributing to the child's sense of power and control, especially when done in front of the child. The obvious solution to this is that parents agree to disagree at times, but *never* in front of the child.

6) Many parents believe that they should never criticize a child because he may develop low self-esteem or inferiority feelings. Without learning to accept criticism, the child may develop grandiosity and start thinking he can never do anything wrong. Also, he may learn never to admit wrongdoing.

7) Parents often dole out punishment that is not consistent with the crime: a) the punishment is too severe and does not fit the bad behavior; b) too much time elapses between the bad act and the punishment; and, c) the child is told to wait until her other parent comes home when the punishment will become more severe. Inconsistent punishment is a prime example of providing the child with a reason to resent you, which justifies her delinquent behavior. Now when she steals from you or hits her sibling, she is only getting even with you.

8) Some parents give the young child complete access to the refrigerator any time throughout the day, thereby satisfying all

demands for food and drink, especially junk food, rather than insisting that the child eat nutritional food during meal times. Parents who do this often feel they were deprived as a child and have promised themselves that their children will not suffer the same deprivation. Children who are taught they will always be given what they want when they want it fail to learn self-control and will misbehave and often embarrass the parents in public.

9) Many middle class parents believe that if they praise their child as smart, attractive, and perhaps stronger than other children, they contribute to positive self-esteem. Such parents do not realize that when you do that with a budding criminal, you contribute to his already over-inflated ego.

10) Another faulty premise parents rely upon is that, since a young child needs protection, it is all right for the parents to lie for him (within reason). When I was five years old, a friend and I were responsible for burning a shed—he gave me the matches and I lit the fire. When police were called, my friend's mother immediately blamed me for the fire. She also screamed at her son to keep his mouth shut. When parents blame others and provide excuses for their child, it reinforces the idea that the child does not need to accept responsibility for his own misdeeds but should instead blame others for them.

11) Many parents, even though they have good intentions, deny that a problem is serious. After all, they reason, many children steal candy from stores at least once or take change from their mother's purse. They fail to see that such acts can become habitual and will require more than just ordinary discipline to correct.

12) Many good parents frequently tell me that if the child steals from a store at a very early age, they will make her go back and return the goods and apologize to the store owner. To reiterate, this technique may be effective with a non-criminal child but not with the budding criminal, first, because such a child does not

believe she is doing anything wrong, and second, because the excitement from stealing far outweighs the embarrassment of being caught. In addition, many defiant children are very good at covering up their deeds and seldom do get caught. The reward from their criminal activity carries a lot more weight than an occasional bit of embarrassment or punishment that a parent may impose.

Some children come from homes where everybody steals—mother, father, brothers and sisters. Children learn by imitation. It is difficult for such a child raised in this environment to grow up not stealing. However, despite this, each individual is responsible for her own actions, and children do come from such backgrounds and grow up to be law-abiding adults, especially if they have a good role model to identify with early in life.

Dr. Samenow, in his book *Before It's Too Late*, suggests that denial is a common defense mechanism used by parents to rationalize or deal with the budding criminal. He reasoned that the adult usually tends to shift the blame from the child to outside forces such as peer group pressure, difficulty in school, or in many cases, to some traumatic experience early in the child's life. Furthermore, he stated when dealing with male children, many parents simply try to attribute the anti-social behavior to a developmental phase fairly common among boys. We all know the expression, *boys will be boys*.

13) Inconsistency in parental discipline provides great opportunity for the budding criminal. She is an expert at manipulation and exploiting disharmony at home. It is not uncommon for such a child to go from one parent to another, or to grandparents, to get what she wants.

Not only parents, but the system frequently fails to understand budding criminal children and reinforces or promotes criminality rather than reducing or eliminating it.

My clinical experience provides too many examples. One mother called me urgently to say that I must see her child, Tommy, because things were escalating out of her control. In our conversation prior to the appointment, she told me that Tommy was already failing third grade. The school specialist had seen him, as well as a teacher from the head office who specialized in behavior problems with children. Next, a social worker was called in to investigate the home, then a psychologist administered a battery of psychological tests, and more recently, an appointment was made with another psychiatrist who wrote a prescription for Ritalin, all because Tommy was diagnosed initially with behavior problems. Tommy was disruptive in class, he was fighting with other students, he was very argumentative with teachers, he demonstrated socially inappropriate behavior and some sexual misbehavior with some of his classmates, including lifting a girl's dress.

The psychological tests indicated that Tommy had above average intelligence, yet seemed somewhat hyper and impulsive. The social worker discovered that there was a lot of tension in the home and Tommy's mother was considering marriage counseling. (The marriage eventually broke-up).

When I arranged to interview Tommy, I found him an attractive child but he initially refused to talk to me. This changed when I decided we would play some games. Each session was divided into 60 percent games and 40 percent counseling which focused mainly on my asking Tommy questions about his life, attitudes, and feelings toward his parents, teachers, and classmates. Even though the child was only eight years old, I could see that much damage had already been done, mainly by the officials designated to help him.

Tommy had already been removed from his classmates and placed in a special class. He was also receiving special tutoring and was being administered Ritalin for Attention Deficit Disorder. The social worker explained to his parents that Tommy was reacting to the tension at home and suggested if the climate at home were to become more stable, some of Tommy's problems would likely disappear.

During the first three months I counseled this young boy, the problem worsened. It became clear I was dealing with a budding criminal. I did notice, however, that Tommy did not demonstrate an attention deficit when we played games he liked such as checkers or chess. In fact, Tommy was able to focus rather well. I suggested that the child's main problems were not that he was hyperactive, suffering from Attention Deficit Disorder, or reacting to the tension at home. Rather, he was a smart little fellow who had decided to do things his own way and use the system to get what he wanted.

Tommy's main problem at school was that he was simply bored. School was not exciting or challenging enough for him. I suggested that everyone, including myself, had misdiagnosed Tommy. Once I realized what we were dealing with, I called Tommy's mother and gave her a new strategy.

I instructed his mother that from that point on, the war should begin. All control had to be taken from the boy—he had considerable control, too much for an eight-year-old. From now on, almost all television privileges were to be cut off; every privilege had to be earned, even small ones. I went to the school and fortunately had complete cooperation from the school principal. I suggested that Tommy be removed from the special education class and be returned to his regular class. In order to lessen the teacher's uneasiness, I volunteered to sit in the class to see that control was maintained.

By this time, Tommy had formed a strong bond with me. I found that, especially in school, he was so anxious to please me he did not exhibit the behavior everyone complained about, especially when I was present. Even the teacher expressed surprise at the change. I also applied techniques used successfully in the past. Whenever he harmed another child or teacher, I planned activities to benefit the injured party. Since I was working primarily within the confines of his school, the principal, who supported my new strategy, agreed not to involve other professionals in Tommy's therapy during this time. I further advised the mother to discontinue his prescription of Ritalin as he was not hyperactive and also to discontinue the psychiatric visits.

Over time, we made much progress, and Tommy became a responsible, empathetic child. At that point, my therapy with him ended. Two years later, I invited Tommy and his mother with her new husband to my home. I was gratified to hear and see that the change in Tommy had become permanent.

Some important lessons may be extracted from my experience with Tommy. Whenever a professional, clergyman, parent, or school teacher makes excuses for a budding criminal child instead of having him face responsibility for his actions, it promotes or reinforces criminal behavior. A hyperactive child, when prescribed Ritalin to reduce his anxiety level, in my experience, simply becomes a more relaxed criminal. Juvenile offenders with drinking problems may be helped to quit drinking, but then we have a sober criminal who is more dangerous and difficult to catch. The same logic would apply to a drug addict. The existence of an addiction is often used as another excuse. I do not believe an addiction has total control over the individual. I have witnessed too many children and adults quit taking drugs and alcohol cold turkey. It is all a matter of their will and attitude towards the addiction.

Finding new ways of dealing with the budding criminal requires change not only for the child but for our whole system. We must realistically view budding criminal children for what they are, determine how they think and then ask what can be done to affect positive changes.

When an adolescent or preadolescent starts having trouble with the police, the police are usually quite realistic. They know instinctively that the kid likes whatever he is doing, and they tend to do what is required under the law and ignore the excuses. However, they continuously have to face professionals and lawyers who block their ability to deal with these young criminals by removing them from our streets.

I do not suggest that the punishment usually employed by the police and rendered by the courts is the best way of dealing with young offenders. However, in many cases as discussed previously, there is no alternative. How else can you prevent continuous damage to others being done by the juvenile offenders except by removing the offender from society?

When a juvenile offender ends up in jail or an institution that tries to teach discipline and attempts to break the subculture, it is frequently too late. When young criminals get together in this kind of setting, they teach one another and directly or indirectly become better criminals.

One of the biggest wastes of effort rigorously used by professionals in such institutions is to spend too much valuable time taking case histories. Case histories among juvenile offenders are very similar and usually provide excuses for why criminal behavior is practiced instead of offering ways to correct it. It makes much more sense to use the available time to get to know the child, identify the criminal traits in that particular individual, and work hard to teach the offender morality, using my or another method which gets results. The alternative—being fixated on the past environment and inherited deficiencies—only leads to a dead end and waste of resources, money, and time.

Currently, the system mostly uses the excuse method in dealing with young criminals. Yet, when a child has trouble reading, she gets extra help in reading; when she has trouble with mathematics, she gets help in mathematics. Likewise, when she shows a moral deficit, she should be taught morality. We may disagree on how to teach morality, but we should all agree that this is a key approach.

One of the biggest myths in the field of psychiatry and social work is that we have to teach children to love themselves so that they can learn to love others. As I've said before, I strongly disagree. Teaching budding criminal children to love themselves will only feed self-centeredness and directly or indirectly reduce their ability to practice moral behavior, that is, consideration and respect of others. As I pointed out in an earlier chapter, parents make serious mistakes in the name of love. If we love a child too much, he thinks he is special and superior to other children. Loving must therefore include teaching a child how to love, which can be shown through expressing feelings of empathy, consideration, and respect for others. However, most of my reading in the field plus my real experience suggests that to achieve self-love you must first learn to love yourself exclusively. Only then can you love others. This is the opposite of learning to love others so you can love yourself.

In the same vein as self-love, teaching the child to have high self-esteem, (a very popular concept especially in the school and social work fields), is again misleading and misunderstood. Most young offenders do not have low self-esteem—they have high self-esteem. Unfortunately, their self-esteem is based on criminal values. When a juvenile offender tells me that he is tough, the implication is that he can beat up any one of his peers, immediately increasing his self-esteem.

The standard explanation in school when a child is not doing well is low self-esteem. Therefore, the child looks for other means of building self-esteem and eventually criminal behavior may satisfy that need. The idea that children need high self-esteem is based on our traditional view of non-criminal children, and we don't realize that when we are not dealing with a normal child the child's needs are very different. He or she is on the way to becoming an irresponsible person. The criminal child does poorly in school not because he has low self-esteem or is incapable of learning—he just doesn't find school as exciting as criminal activity.

Since my belief is that all teaching that contributes to self-centeredness is contributing to criminality, even teaching self-centered self-esteem will do more harm than good. I would like to get rid of the concept of self-esteem altogether. If we ask a good person if he loves himself or if he has high self-esteem, he generally will be embarrassed by the questions. Good people are too busy giving and loving others to worry about how they feel about themselves.

Finally, I want to reiterate my pleas that professionals invest far too much time giving children and adults excuses for their criminal behavior. The most popular excuse accepted and used by almost all journalists, newspaper professionals, school teachers, etc. is child abuse. Again, correlations are not causes. Many abused children do not become criminals. I recently saw a thirteen-year-old child who expressed remorse for hurting his sister, and he told me that he was told by a social worker that because he was abused himself, he is now abusing his sister. I asked him why, if he was abused and has already experienced such pain, he would inflict that pain on his sister. He understood this rationale immediately and expressed remorse. Remorse in the young budding criminal is a positive and necessary feeling.

Some other popular excuses used by professionals to explain away the behavior of budding criminals are: disharmony at home, divorce, single parenting, parents addicted to drugs or alcohol, too much or not enough love, unsupportive family, and lack of discipline. This list can go on and on.

I am always amazed to see a child from a nice middle class family, with well-adjusted brothers and sisters, who is the only one showing delinquent criminal behavior. How does one explain it? I suggest that in many of these cases, this particular child may be treated differently by his parents and school authorities because he is different. As long as we see our budding criminal children as victims, failing to see that they are the victimizers, we will have trouble teaching responsibility and awareness of the effects of their actions on others.

Years ago, six-year-old Jane was brought to my clinic by her adoptive parents, who complained that she demonstrated inappropriate sexual behavior towards other children and her adoptive father. She tried to take boys from her class to the bathroom and engage in sexual activities; she would masturbate in class; her adoptive father complained that she would be sexually aggressive with him, inviting him to have sexual activity and grabbing him.

Because the parents were extremely worried about her, I saw Jane for about forty or fifty sessions. What is surprising about our relationship is that not once did she show inappropriate sexual or any other improper behavior in my company. From the first session, I tried to explain to her that any kind of sexual behavior toward me or other children would be unfair and would be very upsetting to everyone involved. Her adoptive father told me that the school reported a reduction in the frequency of her sexually aggressive behavior. However, he confided that she was still inappropriate with him and he was worried that she would teach her younger brother these habits.

I asked her father to bring me all the records of previous treatments she had received. Apparently, Jane's inappropriate sexuality started at the age of three. As I have already indicated, one of the warning signs of potential criminality is an extremely early interest in sex or inappropriate sexual behavior.

The father also stated that Jane demonstrated other behavior problems, such as lying and stealing. Investigating the case carefully, I discovered that she saw a child psychiatrist at the age of three and was diagnosed with Attention Deficit Disorder with some dyslexia when she started school. I found her to be a bright, fun-loving, friendly young girl. I suggested that the previous focus of treatment had been to try to explain her behavior in terms of some neurological dysfunction. Because she was rather friendly and quite an extrovert, it was easy for me to teach her how her behavior affected others, especially how it affected me. This form of treatment focused on first developing insight and then developing moral behavior.

In our sessions together, she became very anxious to please me, and the sessions, as her parents and teacher later pointed out, indeed achieved their goal. I believe that the earlier focus on Jane's neurological deficit was an attempt to find the cause for her sexually inappropriate behavior. Unfortunately, this wasted valuable years that could have been used more productively by teaching the child moral behavior.

12

Changing the Young Offender

Most people believe criminals are either born or are a product of their environment, and view the jail system as a means to protect the public from the criminal and punish the criminal for his crimes. Criminals are generally viewed as bad people or unfortunate victims of circumstances beyond their control. The justice system tries to rehabilitate many of these criminals with very little success.

Traditional treatment programs for the young criminal attempt to isolate the causes of criminality. Most efforts focus on identifying what happened in the person's life to make them become criminals. The juvenile criminal will tell us unfortunate stories such as: "I was beaten by my father"; "My mother was a prostitute"; "My father was an alcoholic"; or "My friends forced me to join them."

How many of us have also suffered from similar unfortunate childhood experiences, yet have become responsible adults? Perhaps it would be more useful to know that the criminal, early in life, made choices that directly or indirectly led to a life of crime. It is likely that the child who is exposed to unfortunate family experiences may be more prone to committing crimes. However, I believe effective rehabilitation should focus more on the individual's way of thinking and acting, over which he or she has some control, rather than on past social conditions which cannot be changed. In essence, dwelling on the past provides the criminal with an excuse for continuing his criminal behavior. Excuses reduce the likelihood of the young criminal ever taking responsibility for his or her actions.

Many people believe criminals have little conscience and do not feel for others. How could they if they commit these crimes? I have already expressed my opinion that there is only a small population who are incapable of feeling empathy. These individuals require highly specialized treatment programs. I want to suggest again that the majority of criminals are capable of experiencing strong feelings, especially for their loved ones. If these feelings are aroused, they will feel guilt, which provides strong motivation for change. Once this motivation is established, a criminal should be encouraged to engage in activities which are incompatible with crime: consideration for others, helping their family, respecting rules and regulations, community work and helping other criminals to leave the life of crime. The process of change may take considerable time and effort, yet what is the alternative?

The method which I have been describing is the one I have used successfully for changing the criminal child. It can also be applied to children of all ages—from the age of three or four to adolescent seventeen-year-olds. I believe the method is effective with all budding criminals. However, since behaviors vary with greater or less maturity, the way it is applied will vary, depending on the age.

This new method is called for because traditional efforts to change serious behavior problems in children have been largely unsuccessful. In many cases, parents, teachers, and professionals don't understand that in trying to eliminate the undesirable behavior by looking for its causes rather than changing the child, they actually achieve the opposite result and sometimes even promote criminality.

Young criminals are not like other children, as we have previously indicated. They have exaggerated self-centeredness and because of this, traditional methods of punishment and reward have proved ineffective with them. Most attempts to use punishment as a method to change such children's behavior build resentment and provide them with an excuse to continue misbehaving. If you reward young criminals, you only provide them with merit they think they rightly deserve. Only by truly understanding the characteristics of these children can we help them to change.

Recent research findings on some methods that provide promise come from several sources. In his book, *Reality Therapy*, William Glasser emphasizes that delinquency and neurotic behavior are not the results of some psychological maladjustment, rather they are rooted in irresponsible behavior. A person is not irresponsible because he is sick; rather he is sick because he is irresponsible. Thus, for Glasser, initiating responsible behavior is the key to change.

I would like to extend that philosophy to moral behavior and argue that even a young child, if he does not develop a sound moral foundation, will become disturbed. In other words, he is not bad because he is sick, he is sick because he is bad.

I agree with Thornton and Reid, who use a cognitive moral approach to explain criminality, suggesting that delinquent children are stuck at a very early stage on egocentric moral development, which also suggests that *what feels good is okay* and *what feels bad is not okay*. Since such a child is very egocentric, having fun at someone else's expense would be a natural development of such an attitude.

Another important idea comes from Carol Gilligan, who developed the concept of *contextual relativism* which suggests that feeling and obligation to another person are strong motivating forces for many young girls. She demonstrated that young girls generally make moral choices with the consideration of other people in mind.

Finally, there is also a significant spiritual ingredient to the method I feel works best. Cromer, in his article, "Repentant Delinquents: A Religious Approach to Rehabilitation," told a story about Rabbi Reuven Elba who successfully managed to teach spiritual values to young lawbreakers and managed to curb their drift into delinquency. The rabbi claimed to be able to raise feelings of guilt and remorse and secure a promise from the youth not to repeat the same delinquent behavior.

I have already suggested that delving into the causes of criminality is not productive. This activity provides excuses to the young criminal and may even promote the development of criminality. I instead emphasize identifying the young criminal and showing those who care about him what to do (rather than getting lost searching for elusive causes that may only be correlations).

How many times have you been in a restaurant and noticed young children screaming and throwing food on the floor? Parents seem embarrassed, but rather than remove the children from the situation, they try to placate them with treats, promises or giving in. By doing that, the parents are reinforcing the behavior rather than eliminating it. Undoubtedly, this is the wrong approach.

We must examine what can be done to set them on the right course. Depending on the degree of criminality and the degree of self-centeredness (because we identified criminality by the degree of self-centeredness), changing the budding criminal may be quite an arduous undertaking. I believe the following five-point model is very practical, pragmatic and produces good results.

Control

If you are unable to take control away from the young budding criminal, you might as well give up. All other efforts to change him will be wasted. Unfortunately, there is no clear-cut method to gaining control, and specific methods depend on the interaction between the adult and the child.

Here is an example of how you can achieve some control in some children.

With children that exhibit low degrees of criminality and usually try to get control through temper tantrums, time-outs are an effective form of punishment. Once a child is isolated for a period of time, he realizes that the temper tantrum is not accomplishing his goal of gaining control. From a very early age children need to learn that certain rules and regulations are not negotiable.

Non-negotiable actions include going to bed, doing chores, cleaning their rooms, and maintaining table manners. Rules which are negotiable should not give the child the impression that he is in control. These include visiting a friend, inviting a friend to the house, or deciding what kind of movie or television program the child may watch.

When you deal with a budding criminal, control is the most important issue, and if you don't gain control, the battle is lost. It may indeed take a battle to seize control. Let me present one more example from my own experience.

I was called to a school where Peter, an eleven-year-old boy, highly intelligent and aggressive, was destroying books, beating up other children and interrupting the teacher to the point where the teacher was so desperate she was ready to quit teaching. The teacher then approached me. The first thing I did with Peter was to seize control by consistently accompanying him. I sat with him in every class, went home with him to see his parents and spent considerable time with him in my office. I don't know whether Peter respected me or feared me, but I do know I was able to take control right away. Later I used other methods to bring about change in the child.

Excuses

The young criminal is an excuse expert. For example, if he steals, he denies he did it or blames someone else. He says he needed the candy he stole because he was hungry. The adult in charge should refute all rationalizations and explanations for such behavior. The child must be told to tell the truth and take full responsibility for desirable and undesirable behavior.

Excuses come in two varieties: 1) the child makes excuses for himself, and 2) other people make excuses for him (parents, social workers, psychologists, and psychiatrists). The excuses made by professionals will be discussed in a separate chapter.

When a child makes excuses for himself, he will often make his behavior appear to be not only okay, but a noble moral act. This makes his behavior often easy to dismiss. For example: "I stole mittens from my neighbor because my other friend lost his and his hands were cold. The kid I stole from had a lot of mittens 'cause he was rich." While the reason sounds quite noble, the action is obviously incorrect and immoral. This so-called "good" excuse cannot be accepted as reasonable behavior.

The second type of excuse for a child's bad behavior is made by society and psychological professionals. These include claiming the child has low self-esteem, is abused, is unloved, is under peer pressure, or suffers from a psychological or medical problem such as (ADD), dyslexia, etc. These character, intellectual, and background factors may exist and may be correlated with criminality, but they are not direct causes of criminal behavior and do not provide a legitimate explanation for criminality. For instance, for every abused child that becomes a criminal, there may be four or five that do not.

In many of these cases, the problem is not so much the correlation but rather the failure to understand the child and effectively teach morality to that child in the form of empathy, compassion or respect for others.

Problem children who act out in anti-social ways have to be made aware that their behavior is a criminal activity. This process usually involves three stages: 1) understanding, 2) realization, 3) empathy.

Understanding

The small percentage of children, of whom I spoke earlier, who do not understand right from wrong or do not have the capacity to understand right from wrong, demand a more rigorous course. The only effective method of teaching values or pro-social behavior in these cases would be through behavior modification techniques that reinforce desirable behavior and punish undesirable behavior. However, most children have some understanding of right and wrong, and a simple explanation will have some meaning to them, even though they may not accept it.

Realization

By realization we mean that the child becomes aware of his actions and how they affect others. This can be done by constant repetition and example. Let's say that Johnny pushes his sister because she took his favorite toy. One simply has to show Johnny that his action is upsetting to his mother and sister, which will lead to a discussion of more positive ways for him to deal with his sister.

When dealing with an older child (i.e. between the ages of thirteen and seventeen) who is a juvenile offender, I often try to hold a psychological mirror to the child to show him what he is really like—not what he thinks he is like. I do this by reviewing his characteristics with him. Once the characteristics of the criminal child are discussed in detail, surprisingly I find that many of the children can see themselves, if they are willing to admit the truth.

Once the criminal child admits that the portrait I convey of him as the young criminal is accurate, I then focus treatment on teaching the opposite of each trait. In many cases, we start practicing the opposite behavior as soon as some realization takes place. If the child is used to breaking rules and regulations, now he is asked to abide by them. If he shows a disrespectful attitude by the way he talks, argues, or acts during group activities, we show him the proper way of acting and speaking and expect him to start practicing these.

Recently, a young offender asked me, "How can you tell if I am really changing?" I reminded him how he used to act when we first started group therapy. He used to slouch and paid no attention to what was being said, compared to sitting up properly and listening. He used to consistently interrupt, attempting to gain control, but now he was much more respectful. He seemed to appreciate the feedback and it served as reinforcement for his change in attitude.

Empathy

Schulman and Mekler suggested that asking a child how another person feels is sometimes sufficient to obtain empathy. I also show videos and television programs that demonstrate the same effect and use role playing and group discussions to help children whose capacity for empathy has not been developed.

Once a child experiences empathy, we can begin training him or her to be responsible, and improvement in moral behavior follows. From my experience with juvenile delinquents, I have concluded that the earlier we teach a child to practice empathy, the less likely he is to be a repeat offender.

School systems frequently fail to understand budding criminal children and often resort to suspension or other types of punishment as deterrents from future infractions. School personnel use traditional behavior modification methods, not realizing that these children must be handled differently from non-criminal children. Unless we work very hard to impart awareness, empathy, consideration and respect for others, the desired results will not be achieved in a child already acting out in anti-social ways.

Guilt

It is important to teach the young criminal to feel appropriate guilt when he hurts others. As I pointed out before, there is considerable confusion and misunderstanding in earlier research regarding the concept of guilt. With the defiant child, one must clearly distinguish between feelings of guilt that focus on oneself and those that focus on others.

Imparting guilt that focuses on the self is a negative emotion and only leads to anxiety and depression. An example of such guilt may be feeling badly for overeating. However, guilt that focuses on others generally serves as a guide to moral actions. Such guilt provides the motivation that is needed to act in a moral fashion and, in many cases, will lead the criminal child to helping people rather than hurting them.

One of my own experiences is a good example. When I was young, I lived in a village where owning a bicycle was a luxury. When I received my bicycle, I was the only child to have one. In my own form of extortion, I told a friend that if he slapped the face of a child I disliked in the communal dining room of the kibbutz where we lived, I would lend him the bicycle for a half-hour. Sure enough, my friend slapped the boy in the face in front of forty classmates and several teachers.

The repercussions of that activity were devastating for me. The authorities at the kibbutz wanted to send me to reform school. However, my father convinced the pedagogues in the village that he would punish my actions in his own way. First, he made me apologize to the parents of the boy who did the slapping. Then he decided that I would serve as bodyguard for the boy who was slapped, as he was truly victimized in the episode. My father also gave me a long lecture on how unfair it was to hurt another child who could not help himself.

Since I was very strong, I took my job as a bodyguard very seriously. After that incident, no one ever harmed that child again. This story illustrates how empathy and guilt were used positively by my father to teach me a lesson and to protect someone who had been my victim. As far as I can recall, it was the last time I physically hurt anyone.

One dramatic example which highlights the use of guilt is my counseling experience with Joelle, an eleven-year-old blind child who was consistently stealing. Traditional methods of punishment did not change this child's behavior. Her mother told me that other professionals had concluded that the child was stealing to get attention because she felt neglected by her divorcing parents. I would argue that when someone steals, they certainly do not want to attract attention to themselves.

Talking to Joelle made it clear that she loved her mother very much and the last thing she wanted to do was to hurt her. Since Joelle was blind, I asked the mother to come to my session and put water on her face so that the child could touch her tears. This allowed the child to realize and feel the effect her stealing had on her mother. We aroused the child's sense of guilt, and the results were dramatic. After only four sessions, her mother reported that Joelle was no longer stealing and she almost stopped telling lies. Seeing or feeling a mother's tears, a technique I discussed throughout this book, has become one of my most frequently used motivational methods for arousing guilt and empathy.

In one of my group sessions I invited Kate, a mother who was married to a criminal and had two children who also turned out to be criminals, to come to a session and talk about her experiences. Kate had been speaking for a half-hour when I suddenly noticed that two or three juvenile offenders had started to cry.

Again, the use of a dramatic demonstration of hurt is a very effective way of arousing guilt.

Moral Action

We want the young criminal to start doing good things and feeling pride in his positive actions. Since punishment is not effective with criminal children, we can promote behavior change by encouraging these children to engage in activities that involve helping others. I once suggested to a teacher that instead of punishing a difficult eleven-year-old when he did something unfair to another child, she should instead ask him to come up with a program of doing something good for the other child. As he started doing these activities, we saw the child getting high on helping. When one engages in moral activity involving helping others, according to my experience and supporting research, one gets a natural high from it. This approach seems to work well with defiant children.

Due to the characteristics of a criminal child, an activity that is incompatible with these characteristics will sometimes move the child to moral behavior.

Systematic teaching of moral behavior is discussed in detail in the book *Bringing Up a Moral Child* by Schulman and Mekler. It is not a topic I can develop fully in this book, but I offer one very effective technique: sit with the child and help him to design a program of helping others, making sure the child understands that he is responsible for his plan. Keeping in mind that it is extremely important in this process not to allow the child to make excuses if he does not stick with his commitments and always reward him when he takes responsibility for good or bad behavior.

Generally, the more the child engages in activities that show concern and respect for others, the more comfortable he will become with these activities. His sense of self-esteem will then be based on moral activity, and in effect, he may get a high that is incompatible with the kind of high he was getting from irresponsible behavior.

A point clearly described by Glasser in his book, *Reality Therapy*, should be repeated for emphasis—only a responsible individual can teach responsibility. In other words, only a highly moral person can effectively teach values to a child, first because the child will tend to identify with the teacher and second, because the child may cleverly see that the teacher is not practicing what he preaches, thus undermining the process.

I would like to emphasize that when teaching values to children, unless the relationship between teacher and child is built on trust and honesty, the results will be disappointing. Remember, good relationships are built on the adult's capacity to go to the child's level rather than vice versa. Similarly, as I've observed before, when dealing with young criminals, it may be necessary to talk their language.

The older the child and more established the criminal thinking has become, the more difficulty I encounter in reaching the good inside. Respect, compassion, trust, and empathy can be taught to almost any child at an early age. Later this becomes more difficult. Just as in teaching any subject to children, some will learn faster than others and some will be easier to teach than others, but remember, perseverance and consistency can produce successful results in many cases.

The systematic teaching of values or morality has been neglected in our culture in spite of all religious attempts at tackling the problem. Perhaps such teaching must originate in the home.

Finally, the reason why these changes work, I believe, is that the child reduces self-centeredness by practicing consideration and respect for others. It is a very practical approach which avoids the pitfalls of:

a) teaching a child to love himself, which runs the risk of building arrogance rather than self-respect;

b) teaching a child to establish self-esteem, which he may find by being rebellious.

Truly moral people spend little time worrying about how they feel about themselves. Their energy is spent focusing on others which produces both a positive high and good mental health.

You will recall that I discussed an aggressive eleven-year-old boy who almost destroyed a teacher before I managed to take control away from him as a first step toward teaching him empathy and responsible behavior. My second step was to go to his home and spend considerable time with his mother, basically coaching the mother to consistently show the boy how his actions were affecting her.

After several visits, the boy began to see the impact of his unfair acts on his mother. In order to further pursue my idea of moral action, I instructed his teacher that whenever the boy bullied or hurt another child, rather than punish him, the teacher should sit with the child and design activities that he could engage in for the next two weeks—activities in which he could help the child who was initially the victim. Surprisingly, the boy seemed to enjoy that kind of activity. It took only three weeks for him to shift from being a belligerent kid to a highly cooperative teacher-helper. Since the boy was also very bright and had leadership qualities, the teacher was now able to use him to control other children in the class. She was so pleased with the change in the boy's behavior that she became an advocate of my method.

Unfortunately, when the teacher and I shared this case study at a school meeting, the majority of teachers objected to the method. They were more comfortable with traditional approaches that excused the child because he came from a bad home. They felt we needed to correct the bad home before we corrected the child. This theory will be discussed in a later chapter.

When we talk about awareness as part of the strategy for change, we must emphasize again that when dealing with very young children, the characteristics of bad behavior being exhibited should be totally understood by the adult in charge and the main focus should be teaching empathy, respect and consideration for others.

One interesting research study with babies supports this method of creating behavioral change in young problem children. The purpose of the study by Colby *et al.* was to examine the relationship between the mother's behavior and a baby's willingness to help others in distress. Sixteen mothers of babies between the ages of one-and-a-half and two-and-a-half volunteered to take part in the experiment. For a nine-month period they kept a record of all incidents of distress.

Whenever someone in the child's presence expressed painful feelings, caused by either the child himself or by someone else, the child obviously responded to the mother's behavior. The nature of the response was also recorded as soon as possible after the event. The children's responses usually took the form of physical or verbal sympathy, such as *You're feeling better now*; hugs; providing food or toys; or looking for someone else to help the victim.

When the child did not cause the distress, altruistic behavior was observed on 34 percent of occasions and when the child was causing the distress himself, 32 percent of the occasions. Obviously there was a big difference between children.

Also, the mothers' reactions to different situations were analyzed and recorded. Mothers who gave effective explanations to the children, such as, "You see, Doug is crying—don't hurt him because he is very upset" or "I'm upset because you hurt him," etc. produced the highest percentage of spontaneous altruism in babies. Mothers who did not react at all to their children, showing indifference, had children who showed less altruistic behavior.

Because I do believe that many parents confuse giving love with teaching the children how to love, I feel such parents neglect systematic teaching of empathy and consideration for others. Providing an extremely self-centered child with love and empathy without teaching him or her to feel for others only reinforces self-centeredness instead of reducing it, contributing to the child's later criminality.

13

The Significance of Guilt

Since guilt is a very controversial subject and professionals generally view guilt as a negative emotion, I would like to discuss the fact that guilt can actually be a very positive emotion.

Psychiatrists and psychologists generally disagree as to the value of guilt in the development of personality. Maybe some of the confusion is due to the debate over what guilt really is. *Webster's Dictionary* defines guilt as "the state of one who has committed an offense, especially consciously..." or a "...feeling of culpability especially for imagined offenses or from a sense of inadequacy...."

In *The Dictionary of Psychology*, guilt is defined as a "...realization that one has violated either ethical, moral or religious principles, together with a regretful feeling of lessened personal worth."

In both *Webster's Dictionary* and *The Dictionary of Psychology*, the focus is on the "self." The process of focusing on "self," I believe, only leads to depression and what psychologists generally define as neurotic anxiety. However, if we view guilt as a moral feeling, following empathy that is directly associated with hurting another person, such guilt is indeed a guide for moral action and is necessary for social harmony. Such guilt cannot cause depression and anxiety but rather can create closeness with people and may be used as a deterrent in hurting others.

Guilt is frequently associated with punishment and in this manifestation serves no useful purpose except to create anxiety and fear.

Guilt, like empathy, is inherent in human nature. Some children as young as three, four and five clearly demonstrate guilt when they hurt another child or their parents. As a child develops criminal tendencies, he devises a way to block guilt by manipulation, excuses, blaming others, and in some cases drinking and taking drugs.

In the late fifties and early sixties, a successful program for the treatment of young drug addicts emerged which viewed the capacity to feel guilt as a healthy part of the human personality. Mowrer was one of the few psychologists who suggested violation of the conscious, rather than excessive morality, promotes neurotic disturbance. Young children never feel good when they behave badly, which is why they resort to excuses.

I have never seen a child or an adult make an excuse for doing the "right" thing. Yet, many always have an excuse for doing the "wrong" thing.

In Dr. Glasser's *Reality Therapy*, he suggests that delinquent and neurotic behavior is not the result of some psychological sickness, but of irresponsible behavior. I have suggested in my own papers following Glasser's rationale that a person is not "bad" because he is sick but rather the opposite. He is sick because he is "bad." Following that logic, one should encourage children to feel guilty when they do harm to others because such feelings can serve as a very strong deterrent for future harmful activity.

Both empathy and guilt are rooted in the unconscious as well as the conscious. Whenever we violate the simple moral principle of "don't do harm to others," guilty feelings will be produced. If these feelings are not used effectively as a deterrent, focus shifts inward instead of outward, which can lead to depression.

Kohlberg, another psychologist, proposed that a child progresses through a series of six stages in understanding the integration of morality. These stages move from egocentricity to universal morality. If moral values are internalized, meaning that you do what you do because you cannot do otherwise, an individual would be capable of using guilt as a guide for action. When a young child develops from egocentric behavior to pro-social behavior, the shift from external guilt to internal guilt should then occur. Unfortunately, such treatment of guilt is not systematically used in child upbringing.

Hoffman was a big supporter of the use of guilt in raising moral children. He suggested and emphasized that the process of socialization involves systematic teaching of empathy, an obvious prerequisite for guilt.

Shulman and Mekler also suggested that morality can be taught to children using guilt as "a powerful inhibitor of selfish and cruel behavior because it is a natural outcome of hurting someone you feel empathy for." Many professionals who attempt therapy with young children with behavior or delinquency problems almost instantly realize that the children are self-centered. I would argue that self-centeredness blocks awareness of the impact of the hurt these children are inflicting on their victims as well as the people that they claim to love.

Again, the blocking of awareness is aided by excuses. A budding criminal child may blame his young friend or sibling for negative acts he himself commits. As he grows older he may blame his behavior on the environment or his peers, drugs and alcohol, or child abuse. If he does not have a good excuse he can always find a professional who will give him one.

A review of various perspectives on guilt suggests we can clearly distinguish guilty feelings associated with harmful acts toward others (other-oriented guilt). If an individual feels guilty about an action which does not harm others but is in violation of his own standards, that individual might be depressed or suffer loss of self-esteem, whereas if the guilt is unconscious, he might be seeking punishment for a lesser transgression according to analytical theory.

If, however, an individual is able to clearly identify the hurt unjustly inflicted on others, his sense of guilt would serve as a guide for moral action and lead to altruistic behavior, as both McKenzie and Regan have noted. If guilt can serve the useful purpose of being an incentive for altruistic behavior in a non-criminal person, then it is argued that it might serve the same purpose with criminals. Whereas most writers have suggested that sociopaths do not feel guilt, Hammer and Ross contend that they do feel guilty but they develop cognitive strategies to ward off their guilt feelings.

As I've said before, I believe that most children have great capacity for empathy and guilt, but some have more than others. There may be a genetic component to this, as some researchers suggest. However, treatments generally used to deal with behavior problems in children do not facilitate guilt and empathy. Instead they create feelings of resentment in the child.

The problem is that most professionals do not understand defiant children. They do not realize that the source of their misbehavior is in the failure to teach them morality. Rather than foster empathy and guilt, the technique used to eliminate some behavioral problems only promotes the development of criminality and the blocking of guilt.

For example, my own child stole a bottle of makeup when she was six years of age. Quickly, I took my daughter aside, started to cry, and told her I did not want her to grow up to be a thief. She felt very guilty and showed empathy towards me because of our close relationship. It was very hard for her to see her father cry. Three years later, she found a wallet in a shopping mall and promptly gave it to a policeman. She couldn't wait to tell me about this incident. I truly believe that by arousing guilt, I eliminated stealing from my daughter's repertoire probably for the rest of her life.

When I was seven years of age, I had a very close friend named Haron. For some reason, Michael, another friend of mine who was sort of a gang leader, decided to beat up Haron on a regular basis every Friday afternoon, a time when there was no supervision in the kibbutz. I should explain that in the kibbutz, children are raised in collective groups rather than at home with parents.

After ignoring several beatings, I started to feel really guilty for not helping Haron. One Friday afternoon, I put a stop to it by threatening Michael, stating, "I'll beat you up badly if you don't stop beating my friend." Haron never forgot my gesture and we remained friends to the day he passed away.

I can provide countless examples of guilt being used as a deterrent from hurting others.

Dave, age seventeen, a member of one of my groups, told me that since he entered prison, he has not been able to touch his one-year-old child. I asked him if I could witness the next visit from the child and Dave's mother. During the visit, Dave and his family were separated by glass; they were only allowed to communicate via telephone. When I was there, I watched as Dave spoke to his mother and tried desperately to touch his child through the glass. I was so moved by that experience that I started to cry. At the same time, Dave cried. That experience was so powerful that he promised me that he would never again commit a crime for the rest of his life.

Five years have passed and occasionally I check on Dave to see how he is doing. Recently I ran into one of his friends who told me Dave has a good job now; he is in his mid-twenties and has never looked back. I cannot be sure that this experience was the turning point. However, I like to believe that the guilt of not being able to touch his one-year-old child left such an impact on Dave that he made a commitment to change his life.

In another case, a young criminal named Mike told me that he managed to alienate everyone in his family during his criminal history. He is living alone and his closest companion is a German shepherd dog. When he heard my method of changing criminals' behavior, he initially laughed saying, "I'm nobody and I have no reason to quit crime." I told him about another adult criminal who said his dog died from a broken heart when he was doing time in jail. Mike admitted that he felt guilty every time he went to jail because his dog seems to "go a little crazy" staying with Mike's relatives.

I cannot say for sure whether that association with the dog was sufficient incentive for Mike to quit crime. However, each time I have checked with Mike in the last several years, I found him staying out of jail and doing rather well.

About ten years ago, I invited a mother and her son to one of my adult criminal groups after the mother informed me the boy was having problems. The mother had told me her son, Robbie, was unmanageable, had been kicked out of school several times, had been stealing since the age of five or six, and she suspected that he also used drugs. She had tried her best to help Robbie, seeing several social workers and a psychologist in the school system without success. In fact, Robbie had been suspended. I felt that my techniques were radically different from others and might get some results.

However, his mother failed to tell me that Robbie had been violent lately, threatening his younger brother and herself and she was afraid of him. The group session they attended lasted about two hours and the group focused on my method of changing criminal behavior. Since we emphasize empathy, guilt and respect, it did not take long for the group members to observe Robbie's attitude towards his mother.

It was obvious to everyone that the boy was on a huge power trip and concepts like empathy, guilt and respect were completely unknown to him. His mother was a good friend and has been keeping in touch with me for the last ten years. Robbie is now twenty-five and doing time in an institution. He has spent more time in jail in the last ten years than outside, in spite of much psychiatric help. When you see no evidence of guilt and very little respect, especially towards the parents, the lack of result from treatment is quite predictable.

For the last twelve years I have been applying my method in group therapy programs in jail. It has been my experience that the majority of juvenile offenders attending my group do not feel guilty. Recently, instead of emphasizing guilt, I have tried to emphasize respect. Even though I have had success using my method, too many of the juvenile offenders progress to adult jail. The ones who do, I've observed, have lost the capacity to feel empathy and guilt.

14

The Significance of Teaching Empathy and Responsibility

As I have emphasized throughout this book, in the last twenty years of my work with criminals I have become almost totally convinced that empathy may be the most important ingredient in the development of moral, social behavior in children, while lack of empathy or failing to develop empathy may be the most important common element in the development of risk behavior in children.

Empathy is the ability to put yourself in someone else's shoes and to feel what he or she feels. If someone feels joy, you feel joy; if he feels sorrow, you feel sorrow. Empathy differs from *sympathy*, which is simply feeling sorry for someone.

One poignant example of how empathy can be used to change behavior is an experience I had with my little friend Jason. He was only two-and-a-half years old and was sitting on the floor carefully and methodically building a castle with dominoes. I joined Jason on the floor and began making my own castle from the dominoes. I wasn't as methodical, so I was able to build more quickly. Before long, my castle dwarfed Jason's. When Jason realized how big my castle was, he used one sweeping motion to destroy it.

His parents were watching from a distance. I signaled to them to stay quiet and not interfere. I asked Jason if he was truly my friend. He said, "Yes." Then I looked at him with tears in my eyes, saying, "Then how could you destroy my castle? What kind of a friend are you?" Jason listened to me, then destroyed his own castle and immediately rushed to help me build an even bigger castle. I think this is a classic demonstration of inherent empathy in small children.

Another example of eliciting empathy has been reported by Eisenberg and Strayer. An eight-year-old boy, after several weeks of joining his friends in harassing black children, started realizing that one of the kids they taunted was kind and polite. Not long after his realization, he saw several of his friends calling the boy "dirty nigger" and pushing him. He went over and broke up the fight. His former friends yelled at him, "You're as crazy as he is." In front of everyone, he told the black boy, "I'm sorry" and continued to apologize.

When the boy was asked by his teacher why he had an attitude change, he said that he felt that the kid, no matter how much abuse he took, was still a good kid. It is obvious that the white boy experienced distress, empathy and guilt.

In one study of empathy, Kaplan reported that at nine months of age, Hope, a little girl, had tears in her eyes when another child fell or cried. In many cases she would cry herself when seeing other babies in distress.

Recall the earlier example of Michael, age fifteen months, and his friend Paul who were fighting over a toy. Paul started to cry. This disturbed Michael and he let go, but Paul continued to cry. Michael then decided to get his own teddy bear and give it to Paul. Paul continued crying. At that point Michael decided to get Paul a security blanket, and when he gave it to the other child, Paul stopped crying.

As I have pointed out in this book, empathy is an inherent human trait and is the basis for moral and social harmony. However, it is important to realize that the capacity for empathy or the ability to develop or learn empathy is not the same in everyone. This explains why some children are more moral than others. Even though there are individual differences among children in their capability to feel for others, that should not deter us from teaching each of them empathy. Such teaching should start as early as age two or three. After all, we do not stop teaching children to read or to add just because some have more difficulty than others.

I strongly believe if you begin teaching children empathy systematically at a very early age, starting at two or three, you will likely prevent development of the budding criminal characteristics I discussed earlier.

I also believe that guilt focused on others rather than self—another important component of character building—and altruism can only develop if empathy is present.

A situation which illustrates the use of these two emotions to correct faulty behavior occurred after Helen, a client, recently told me that her three-year-old daughter, Sally, was consistently being aggressive with other children. Helen had tried a number of the usual deterrents such as "time-out" and taking Sally's toys away. However, Sally's aggressive, abusive behavior toward other children did not stop. I suggested that when Sally was aggressive again, Helen should sit in front of her and show how the behavior was affecting her. How? Show distress and tears. She tried this with dramatic results. Helen used empathy and was able to change Sally's aggressive behavior.

What are the consequences of failing to develop empathy? In a very young child, such failure generally leads to what psychologists call behavior problems. Such a child can become aggressive, manipulative, and use excessive crying, screaming, and other annoying behaviors to have their demands satisfied. As the child grows up, he may become a bully at school. His whole life and mode of operation becomes, *I'm number one and I'm going to look after number one.* He has little respect and consideration for his peers, brothers, sisters, or parents. He may cry when he gets hurt or when he is in distress. However, this is not empathy. It is simply an expression of self-pity—the budding criminal is sorry for himself.

Among the many bizarre and outrageous crimes committed by children in the last ten years, the common element appears to be lack of empathy. Now, is acting out violently a psychological disorder or a mental illness? Not really. It is simply the result of failing to develop empathy. Without empathy, human society cannot survive.

Society generally feels very disgusted and upset when adults commit sex crimes. They don't realize that sex crimes are also commonly committed by children. Again, such crimes committed by children are symptoms of a lack of empathy, failure to develop empathy, and utter disregard for another human being. A child who seeks pleasure at the expense of another, whether through sex or violence, is deriving pleasure from the power he exercises over others. The value of another human being is totally unimportant to him.

I once interviewed Charles, an adolescent who brutally assaulted another boy. Charles spoke with pride about how easy it had been for him to commit the act. He felt that he was totally justified because the other child was in special custody, which is usually used by the authorities to separate mainstream criminals from deviant inmates such as sex offenders, or those in danger from other prisoners.

Psychologists generally tend to emphasize understanding of moral values or cognition, and they frequently fail to understand and teach morality of the heart (a concept which is strongly advocated by some feminists). It is my opinion that knowing right from wrong hardly ever serves as a deterrent to immoral acts.

I strongly believe that only if a child *feels* the pain of a distressed victim will he be able to truly develop intrinsic morality and do good because he believes in it, rather than out of fear of punishment or desire for a reward.

In my work with the school system I have counseled bullies, thieves, and liars. I consistently emphasize that change must begin with control and empathy. In every case, I systematically begin with asking the mother (if the child has an active maternal parent) to demonstrate in a dramatic fashion how much pain her child is causing her. Some mothers find it difficult to do. Naturally, some of the children also have difficulty admitting what they have done to cause pain for others.

However, if we have cooperation from parents, teachers and other professionals involved with problem children, we have a much better chance to get the change in attitude and actions we are all seeking.

Although in the last ten years I have seen some juvenile offenders who show almost no evidence of empathy and who sometimes show the opposite—apathy—or even seem to despise their victims, I remain convinced that the innate capacity for empathy is there. In speaking of the children who do not appear to have this important concomitant for moral feeling, Dr. Robert Hare in his book, *Without Conscience*, suggests the use of the term *psychopath*. This is based on the observation that these children seem to be almost totally indifferent to the feelings of pain or hurt in others.

Personally, as I've said before, I do not like the term *psychopath* applied to children, for two reasons. First, when one discusses psychopaths, one really is describing people who exhibit extremes of sadistic behavior, like Charles Manson, Jeffrey Dahmer or more recently the Canadian couple, Paul Bernardo and his wife, Karla Homolka. Second, even though some children show behaviors and affects that may be consistent with the term *psychopath*, such as lying, resentment of authority, stealing, aggressiveness, violence, bullying, hurting animals, senseless vandalism and precocious interest in sex or even murder, these children surprisingly at times also show the ability to feel for others, once the technique I have been advocating is applied.

I believe that conventional psychiatry and clinical psychology are, to a large extent, based on psychoanalytic theory which assumes that most abnormal neurotic and criminal behavior is rooted in a conflict between the conscience or moral restriction (the superego) and the instinctual drive (the id). The failure to resolve that conflict results in maladaptive, acting-out, criminal behavior. Satisfaction of the basic drive and instinct without hurting others is one of the objectives of achieving mental health.

William Glasser's book, *Reality Therapy*, suggests that such a theory is very difficult, if not impossible, to practice when dealing with delinquents who exhibit antisocial behavior. He suggests that responsibility is a key to the rehabilitation of these young people. Glasser defines responsibility as "the ability to fulfill one's needs and to do so in a way that does not deprive others of their ability to fulfill their needs." This, he feels, is the cornerstone of mental health. I agree. Only a moral person can be responsible and healthy and, consequently, an immoral person is irresponsible and sick.

William Glasser's approach to treatment is based on first establishing a relationship with the client. When I started working with criminals, I tried to apply Dr. Glasser's method with some success, but I discovered that before I could teach responsibility, I had to focus on empathy. The reason is that the young criminal's needs are selfish and completely self-centered, and satisfaction of those needs usually ends up in violation of other people's needs and rights. In other words, juvenile delinquents, especially those who are very young, may not intend to hurt others, yet they generally end up doing so.

Therefore, before we can teach responsibility and respect for others, we must teach empathy. Once empathy has been established, we can proceed with teaching responsibility. In a sense, my theory is a precursor of applying William Glasser's theory, especially when dealing with youngsters who are budding criminals.

However, once empathetic feeling is established, Dr. Glasser's theory of teaching responsibility is the next important step in civilizing the budding criminal. According to Glasser, our psychiatric clinics and mental hospitals, as well as our streets, are filled with people who haven't learned or have lost the ability to live responsible lives. Our first job, I believe, is to teach such people (the younger, the better) to show moral feeling and to be empathetic. Once this is successful, we can begin teaching that person to act more responsibly.

Of course, as Glasser points out, ideally children learn "by means of a loving relationship with responsible parents. In addition, responsibility is taught by responsible relatives, teachers, ministers and friends with whom they become involved." But when children do not learn these lessons early, for whatever reason, whether it be parental inadequacy, the environment, or their own constitutions, , we must still not give up and try to impart them.

During moral cognitive therapy, we must try by teaching and retraining to accomplish what is missing in the budding criminal child: empathetic feeling and responsible behavior.

Sometimes when empathetic feeling is established, responsible behavior spontaneously begins. If not, the child must be given limits and led to a new pattern of behavior. When the child behaves rightly, she or he should be praised by the therapist and other responsible adults for acting responsibly. When the child does not act responsibly within limits set, these involved adults should exhibit disapproval and apply disciplinary measures such as removing privileges.

Glasser points out, as I also have seen, that delinquents may resist therapy. This is why control, which I explain in another chapter, is a vital first step in the successful treatment of budding child criminals. Resistance must be met by steady pressure from involved adults on defiant children, guiding them toward empathy and then responsibility. Focus on the present. The past cannot be changed, and the future is unknown. Whatever the reasons are that have made the child what she or he is are far less important than letting the child know he or she must act responsibly now. Our goal is that, over time, as the child acts responsibly and grows up, we can gradually give over the reins of control so that the once budding or juvenile criminal takes on increasing responsibility. Once she or he has learned empathy, that formerly defiant explosive child can become a mature, caring adult.

To effect this change it is most important, Glasser stresses and I believe, that the adults coaching the child have a unified, consistent approach to applying discipline and showing warmth and affection. The other important element is that no excuses are to be accepted for cruel or irresponsible acts and they are not to be glossed over. We must provide a therapeutic program in which the child learns to be caring and then responsible and to continue his or her progress by conforming to sensible rules.

Strict, consistent and fair rules are an absolute necessity if we are to change the defiant, hostile, irresponsible child into an empathetic, solicitous, responsible one.

15

Utopia or Reality

In the last twenty years of my work with criminals, (both young and old as well as "budding"), I have come to believe that the majority of people do have the capacity to develop good moral sense. I have attempted during this book to define morality in terms of the discrepancy we see between the self-centeredness of budding criminals and the respect for others we see in non-criminal children. This means that the more self-centered a person is, the less he is able to love and respect others. The less self-centered a person, the more moral he or she can become.

Twenty years ago, I heard a lecture I will never forget by Dr. Viktor Frankl, a psychiatrist who is also a survivor of a concentration camp. Dr. Frankl suggested that the eye can only look outside. We do not have x-ray vision. Morality is looking outside. The ultimate aim of a moral person is truly liberation from self. Unfortunately, almost all psychological theory of the last fifty years directs people towards examination of "self."

Today, many books displayed in bookstores exhort the importance of focusing on oneself with titles like *The Virtue of Selfishness, How to Look After Number One* and *How to Build Self-Esteem,*

Self-Worth and Self-Respect. I strongly believe that such references to the primacy of "self" are detrimental to the development of morality.

Some psychologists try to say that you have to start by loving and knowing yourself before you can love others. It's been my experience with criminals that one cannot develop moral character by learning to love oneself. Instead, I believe only by loving others may one love oneself.

Many teachers and social workers and some psychologists are endeared to the concept of self-esteem. They do not understand that criminals' self-esteem is based on different values. A criminal who respects a bank robber often despises a sex offender. Both people are hurting other people and certainly hurting their families.

If we are to diminish the numbers of young criminals, we must begin to teach morality very early, beginning at age two. I do not blame parents or society completely for producing criminals. However, I believe that once we know a little bit about the nature of criminality and how it develops, we do not need to know why. We don't need to know why some children learn to read faster than others—perhaps it is intelligence. Just because one child is slightly slower than another, does it mean the teacher will neglect teaching the slower child?

If we understand that morality is focusing outside oneself and is a process of liberation from self, then we can start teaching morality to very young children. By helping them to share, respect others, and most importantly, feel the pain and joys of others, we start them on the way to living moral and satisfying lives. This is the essence of our humanity.

The ability to liberate from self is directly related to the commitment one makes to a cause outside the self. The more we are able to take a child and direct him towards causes outside the self by teaching him to share and to love others rather than himself and to respect his peers and his parents, the more we help him to become a moral and healthy child.

Happiness that is based on self-indulgence never lasts! Happiness based on helping others is the essence of spirituality and can only be achieved if we learn to love and care for others.

I totally agree with Dr. Glasser that a man is not sick because of some mysterious psychological illness—he is sick because he is irresponsible, or, using my terminology, he is sick because he is immoral.

Too many people believe that we can only teach by using extrinsic reward, which some people may call bribery. (If we want to be more sophisticated, we might call it positive reinforcement.) Instead, I believe that we raise moral children when they are motivated by intrinsic processes, meaning doing good because it is the right thing to do, rather than because of what's in it for them.

Philosophers who suggest that altruistic behavior is basically another form of self-interest ignore the fact that there are many moral people who show altruistic behavior, even at the risk of losing their lives. In an interesting experiment, a group of children ages seven and eight received rewards for donating to another child or were fined for not helping. They seemed to be less likely to explain their own behavior in terms of intrinsic motivation to help than children who received no reward at all.

In another experiment, children divided into two groups were encouraged to give away some of their playthings to their peers. After donating, one group was told that they were kind and nice, while the second group was given a prize. Afterwards, children from the first group seemed to share more than the second group. Thus, you do not have to reward a child to teach him intrinsic morality. You just have to help him practice loving behavior, and the development of morality will become spontaneous and natural.

I propose that moral education should be a requirement at all school levels—nursery school, elementary school, high school, college/university. Obviously, we are not going to teach morality to a high school student the same way we do to a grade school child. The curriculum should be designed carefully, based on our present knowledge of instilling moral development by age-appropriate methods.

There are psychologists who are well known in the field of moral development, such as Jean Piaget who wrote *The Moral Judgement of the Child* and Lawrence Kohlberg, the author of *Moral Stages and Moralization*. These men provided very extensive research on the development of morality in children. My proposal for introducing moral education in the school system is based, to a large extent, on Kohlberg's ideas. Dr. Kohlberg suggests that children develop from a pre-conventional type of morality (level one) to conventional morality (level two). On level two, the child does not understand morality but instead associates right and wrong with rules and authority. For example, if you ask such a child, "Why is it wrong to hit your sister?" he will tell you, "My parents say it's wrong and they'll punish me," rather than, "It is wrong and will hurt my sister."

Many adolescents, particularly criminal adolescents, and even some adults never move beyond level two morality. This can be seen in the criminal adolescent who knows that crime is wrong, but doesn't know why and in the adult who believes there are rights and wrongs because society says so.

Post-conventional morality (level three) is based on understanding the universal principal of morality. Those who have reached level three believe in human rights and know that hurting another person is wrong because it is a violation of their rights. This level of morality is reached by few adults and even fewer children or adolescents. Although I believe Kohlberg's theories are invaluable, I find fault with his method because it ignores the emotional aspect of morality which I call moral feeling. It is the instilling of moral feeling which I believe is most important. Again, this theory is advanced by the feminist movement and Dr. Gilligan.

Using Kohlberg's and Gilligan's theories plus my own, we should design a new curriculum for our school systems. By emphasizing the feeling aspect of morality, we may even show children how to progress directly to intrinsic morality and prevent them from stalling at the stage of extrinsic morality. Children will learn to do the right thing because they feel it's not right to hurt another human being, rather than because they may be punished for it or receive a reward for helping someone.

The opposite of hurting is helping. That aspect of morality can be taught to toddlers. When a child engages in certain repetitive activity, the activity eventually becomes natural and spontaneous. Since all children are born with the capacity for empathy and selfishness, we must spend a lot of energy and time teaching them to help and be empathetic, rather than the opposite.

Realizing that some children come from abused and neglected homes while others come from emotionally nurturing homes, it is obvious that not all parents have the time and skills to teach good moral values. I believe that knowing the warning signs and understanding some of the principles discussed in this book may help some parents as well as teachers, counselors, and others involved with our youth to prevent the development of criminality.

I advise parents that, even if they do not see all seven warning signs in their very young children, attacking any one sign (if done with vigor and persistence) can eliminate a lot of problems later. I would also like to believe that professionals, rather than continuing to argue about the best method to teach morality, will agree to foster these important values in their young clients and pupils.

As an example, the Ten Commandments provide universal principles of all religions and all cultures and these can be used as a guideline for teaching proper moral values.

I would like to add another commandment: Respect Your Children. Parents who constantly talk about disciplining their children and who do not understand the values of love, empathy and respect are also missing the point.

Some people may feel pessimistic about budding criminal children and say, "What can I do?" especially if they missed instilling values in these children during their early years. Some believe that the character of a person is formed during the first five years of life and there is nothing much we can do after that time. Much traditional psychological literature supports that view.

Freud was perhaps the most influential, suggesting that human beings' psychological development is determined in the first five years of life. Clarke and Clarke challenged that notion and suggested that there was considerable research to show that we can change people at any age. I would suggest that teenage offenders and even some adults can change if the method I am advocating is used consistently. I have seen it happen in my own work.

Remember that children are born neither good nor bad! Each has a genetic disposition. The direction in which children develop is based on what free choices they make and the influences of their environment. The interaction of these two developments can move the child in positive or negative directions. The more we put weight on these two factors' roles in changing a budding criminal into a morally healthy child, the more likely we will achieve desirable results.

Pro-social behavior in very young children can be taught by practicing. I advise parents and teachers to encourage children to do volunteer work. The teaching of pro-social behavior in early grades could be part of the curriculum in moral teaching. This could involve taking children to retirement homes and nursing homes to engage in helpful behavior. In one experiment in western Canada where hard-core criminals were made Big Brothers to help retarded children, the results were dramatic. Such programs should be used consistently in the correctional system.

Ideally, all parents regardless of economic status should attend formal courses on how to be better parents. I can't think of a more responsible job than raising moral children, yet how many of us ever received education in this area? Even if we do, how many authorities and books on the subject just confuse us because they are not clear in showing us what to do?

What I am suggesting may be a Utopian notion at this point, but it can become a reality. Right now, it costs approximately $100,000 per year to keep an adolescent in jail. The savings to society would be enormous if we invested more money in educational programs for parents, teachers, professionals and others involved with young people which teach how to instill moral values in children. We must start focusing on preventing the development of criminality rather than waiting until children become full-blown criminal adolescents and adults, for we are paying what is, in both human and economic terms, an enormous price.

Appendix A

Small Criminal Attitude Inventory (Ages 3 to 5) Questionnaire

Read each scenario and picture your child in the situation described. Select the answer that best reflects how your child would react.

1. You take your toddler to a restaurant. He refuses to eat his meal, wanting ice cream instead. You say "no." His response is:
   (a) He accepts your "no" gracefully.
   (b) He accepts the "no" after a brief complaint.
   (c) He screams, gets into an argument with you and eventually gives up.
   (d) He screams and screams, throws a temper tantrum in the restaurant and expects you to give up and let him have the ice cream.

2. You take your child to a department store. When you pass the Toy Department, he decides he wants a big, shiny toy truck. You say "no." His response is:
   (a) He accepts your "no" without complaint.
   (b) He accepts the "no" after a brief protest.

(c) He gives up after considerable screaming and arguing.

(d) He causes a scene, hoping you give in and buy the truck.

3. You are putting your child to bed after telling him the promised bedtime story. He then:
(a) Goes to bed peacefully.
(b) Goes to sleep after fussing for a short time.
(c) Refuses to go to bed, screaming and protesting loudly.
(d) Throws a temper tantrum and refuses to go to bed, expecting you to bribe him in some fashion.

4. At nursery school, the teacher asks the children to color pictures for ten minutes. Your child:
(a) Enjoys the task.
(b) Starts complaining and becomes restless after five minutes, but continues coloring for the full ten minutes.
(c) After five minutes, doesn't want to color anymore. He tries to manipulate a classmate to do the coloring for him and demands his teacher's attention.
(d) After two minutes, refuses to color anymore. He protests loudly and claims to have a tummy ache, wanting special attention from his teacher.

5. You take your child to the grocery store and he wants a chocolate bar. You say "no." He reacts by:
(a) Accepting the "no" quietly.
(b) Showing his displeasure but still accepting "no."
(c) Whining and asking why he can't have the chocolate.
(d) Screaming as loud as he can—after all, he deserves to get the chocolate bar right now!

6. You run out of waffles (your usual Saturday breakfast food). You attempt to replace waffles with cereal which your child likes less. Your child:
(a) Eats the cereal without too much complaint.
(b) Complains a bit but still eats the cereal.

(c) Really complains, but if you insist, he reluctantly eats the cereal.

(d) Totally refuses to eat the cereal, screaming and carrying on. There is nothing you can do to make him eat the cereal (short of bribery).

7. You take your child to a fast food restaurant. You order a hamburger and fries, plus a small pop for both of you. Next to you is a father with his daughter, having the same meal with a "large" pop. Your child asks for a "large" drink, too. You have already paid for the small one and refuse to change. Your child:

(a) Accepts your choice.

(b) Protests a bit and asks why the other girl can have a large pop.

(c) Starts complaining but eventually drinks the small pop.

(d) Gets very angry, screams, and throws the small pop on the floor and ends up drinking nothing.

8. At day care or school the teacher reads a story for about fifteen minutes. Your child:

(a) Listens attentively.

(b) Starts getting restless after ten minutes.

(c) Starts disrupting the story after ten minutes.

(d) Screams and carries on, demanding the teacher's full attention after five minutes.

9. The child has been playing a construction game with blocks before bedtime. You ask him to pick up his blocks. Your child:

(a) Does it quickly and quietly and goes to bed.

(b) Takes a long time to pick up the blocks.

(c) Protests about picking up the blocks and ends up hiding some of them under the sofa instead of picking them all up.

(d) Simply refuses to pick up the blocks and gets very angry because you asked him to do it.

10. A new teacher has joined the children on the playground. She

makes recess a lot more fun and the children, especially your child, have really taken to her. At the end of recess, the regular teacher tells all the children to return to class. Your child:

(a) Returns quickly.

(b) Takes some time to return to class.

(c) Is the last to return to class.

(d) Refuses to go to class, forcing the regular teacher to go outside to look for him.

11. At the end of nursery school, you come to pick up your child. Your child:

(a) Is very happy to see you.

(b) Goes with you with some hesitation.

(c) Tells the teacher he doesn't want to go home, which embarrasses you.

(d) Carries on and refuses to go with you, forcing you to carry him out to the car while he screams.

12. You take your child to a department store to buy a toy for Christmas. You aren't rich, so you steer your child to different toys that you can afford. Your child:

(a) Politely points to the GI Joe you showed him.

(b) Decides he would like a small car that's a little more expensive.

(c) Picks a very expensive motorized plane.

(d) Jumps from toy to toy, unable to decide which toy he would like. He quickly manages to frustrate you while he plays with every toy and throws them on the floor when he's through.

13. Your child's report from school usually says:

(a) He is co-operative, friendly and relates well to other children.

(b) He is generally easy to manage, yet at times he gets into minor conflicts with other children.

(c) He is constantly complaining about the work he has to do and complains that other children get more attention from the teacher.

    (d) He is a bully, pushing and hitting other children, especially during recess.

14. You happen to be talking to two of your neighbors because your child frequently plays with their kids. One neighbor has a small cat and dog. The following scenario emerges:
    (a) Your child seems to like the animals and tries to pet them.
    (b) Your child only likes the dog and is mean to the cat.
    (c) Your child seems to dislike both the cat and dog and pays no attention to them.
    (d) Your child is seen several times pulling the cat's tail, laughing and victimizing the dog, either kicking it or throwing objects at it.

15. Your child has a good variety of toys. He:
    (a) Respects the toys and never intentionally breaks them.
    (b) Is sometimes rough with his toys when he is tired.
    (c) Is protective of his toys but has no problem breaking other children's toys.
    (d) Tends to break toys, his own and others'.

16. Your child sees his sister upset or hurt. He:
    (a) Tries to comfort her.
    (b) Seems distressed, but does nothing.
    (c) Seems indifferent.
    (d) Seems to enjoy seeing her hurt and laughs at it.

17. Your child breaks an expensive lamp, yet, no one actually saw him doing it. He:
    (a) Freely admits breaking it when asked.
    (b) Denies it initially but then admits it later when pressed on the matter.
    (c) Keeps denying he broke it without changing his story.
    (d) Denies it and blames it on someone else.

18. You catch your child bringing home candy from the grocery store

that you know he has not paid for. When you talk to him about it, he:
(a) Confesses that he stole it and shows quite a bit of remorse.
(b) Admits stealing but does not seem too concerned about it.
(c) Denies the stealing.
(d) Denies stealing the candy and suggests that his friend from school gave him the candy.

19. The teacher telephoned you one evening, very upset, suggesting that your child hit another child very hard with a toy and caused bleeding. Talking to your child about it, she:
(a) Confesses the fight and makes no excuse.
(b) Admits the fight but says it was self-defense.
(c) Denies the fight altogether saying the teacher was mistaken and that it was another child fighting.
(d) Denies the fight suggesting that she saw the other child fall against the corner of a table.

20. Your child returns from playing with a neighborhood child and has a black eye. You telephone your neighbor and she tells you your daughter was injured as a result of instigating the fight and that her daughter was only defending herself. When you ask your daughter about the incident, she:
(a) Confesses she started the fight, verifying what the neighbor said.
(b) Admits she started the fight but claims she did not deserve such a beating because she only pushed her friend.
(c) Says that the neighbor child called her bad names and she had no choice but to hit her.
(d) Says that the neighbor child hit her for no reason whatsoever before she decided to defend herself.

21. Your child returns from school with earrings you didn't buy and she can't afford. You ask her about them. She:
(a) Confesses she stole them and shows remorse.
(b) Admits she stole them but rationalizes it by saying her friends have so many earrings.

(c) Denies stealing the earrings.

(d) Denies it and says her friend gave her the earrings.

22. As far as you can tell, your child:

(a) Never steals.

(b) Does not steal habitually, but may have done so once or twice.

(c) Steals on occasion.

(d) Steals frequently.

23. Stealing habits of your son or daughter are:

(a) Your child never steals.

(b) He has stolen a few things in the past from strangers.

(c) He steals occasionally from strangers, stores and mom's purse.

(d) He steals from everyone including friends, family and strangers.

24. Your child likes to play with the baby-sitter. Sometimes the baby-sitter has to do some homework. Your child resents her spending time doing things other than playing with her. Your child:

(a) Allows her baby-sitter to do homework, even though she resents it.

(b) Annoys the baby-sitter while she tries to do her homework.

(c) Insists that whenever the baby-sitter does homework, she stop and instead play with her.

(d) Creates scenes that demand her baby-sitter's attention, doing her best to prevent her from doing her homework.

25. Your child's reaction when asked to do any type of chore is:

(a) Co-operative.

(b) Somewhat co-operative but with complaint.

(c) Unco-operative.

(d) Refuses to do any type of chore, says "no" to everything, and screams if there is any attempt to force him or her to do it.

SCORING:

Count the number of A, B, C, and D answers. Give yourself zero points for each A answer, 2 points for each B answer, 3 points for each C answer, and 4 points for each D answer.

If your child scores from 75-100, you have trouble on your hands! If he scores 50-74, there are some difficulties that can be overcome with proper teaching. If he scores 25-49, I would not be too concerned—he is just a normal child. 0-24, you have an angel!

Appendix B

Middle Childhood Criminal Attitude Inventory (Ages 10-12) (Parent Questionnaire)

Read each scenario and picture your child in the situation described. Select the answer that best reflects how your child would react.

1. Your child asks for a video game because his buddy just received one. You explain that the budget for this month does not allow it and perhaps he might get one next month. The child:
   (a) Will be happy to get it at all.
   (b) Complains, saying he needs it now and can't wait.
   (c) Makes a big fuss over the wait.
   (d) Suggests he will find another way of getting it.

2. You take your child to see a movie at the theatre. You refuse to buy popcorn, a large soda and candy. Your child:
   (a) Accepts it.
   (b) Accepts it reluctantly, complaining.
   (c) Makes a lot of noise to embarrass you.
   (d) Causes such a scene that you are very embarrassed and have to leave the theater.

3. Your child asks for a new mountain bike since all his friends seem to have one. Unfortunately, you cannot afford to buy him a new bike at this time. He:
   (a) Accepts this gracefully.
   (b) Accepts this with some minor complaint.
   (c) Objects loudly, using bad language towards you.
   (d) Uses profanity, telling you he will have to find another way of getting the bike (the implication is quite clear).

4. Your child asks for an increase in his allowance. You tell him he must do additional chores at home to earn the increase. He:
   (a) Accepts your offer and willingly does more chores.
   (b) Accepts your offer with minor complaint, saying his friends do fewer chores and get more allowance.
   (c) Refuses to do any extra chores, saying that his friends get more allowance for less work.
   (d) Argues vigorously about your request and suggests he is tired of living in such an unloving home.

5. You take your child to a restaurant, telling him there is a $10.00 limit on what he can order. He wants a large pizza and large pop which amounts to $15.00. You refuse, suggesting that if he wants pizza he'll have to order a small one to stay under $10.00. He:
   (a) Accepts your idea and order a small pizza.
   (b) Accepts it, complaining.
   (c) Accepts it but makes you feel guilty by saying that his friends can order anything they want in a restaurant.
   (d) Gets really angry, refuses to eat anything at all and makes sure almost everyone in the restaurant hears him.

6. You are trying to set a new curfew at 9:00 P.M. rather than 10:00 P.M. for your twelve-year-old. Your child:
   (a) Agrees without an argument.
   (b) Agrees with some argument.
   (c) Gets into many arguments.
   (d) Refuses to accept the curfew stating that all her friends stay out until 10:00 P.M.

7. Your twelve-year-old's bedroom is very messy. You ask her to clean it and tidy her things. She says:
   (a) "No problem."
   (b) "I will do it but I don't see why I have to—it's my room!"
   (c) "I have a right to live my life the way I want to and you can't make me clean my room!"
   (d) "You have no right to force me to clean my room. I like it this way. If you want me to do it, I won't have time until the weekend." (It's clear she does not intend to clean it.)

8. Your son wants to watch a restricted movie (sex and violence) on TV. You say no! He says:
   (a) "OK."
   (b) "OK, but my friend is allowed to watch it, so why can't I?"
   (c) "OK." (However, he watches it anyway.)
   (d) "I've seen worse movies than this. If you won't let me I'll go to my friend's and watch it. His parents are cool, not strict like you."

9. You receive a call from the school principal, stating that your child is continuously causing difficulty in the classroom, particularly in art class. When you ask your child about this, he:
   (a) Confesses to being disruptive and promises he will try to improve his behavior.
   (b) Admits that he has misbehaved but blames it on the boring class—he prefers mechanics.
   (c) Denies it altogether, saying the teacher is confusing him with another boy.
   (d) Says he finds most classes boring and would like to quit school as soon as he can.

10. You receive an urgent telephone call from the police. Your son has beaten up another boy in his class and the school had to call them. When you arrive at the school to get your son, you ask him what happened. He:
    (a) Admits that he got into a fight.

(b) Admits to the fight but suggests it wasn't a big deal as he and his friend were just having fun.

(c) Claims it was self defense.

(d) Blames the fight on the other boy who was calling him names and making fun of him.

11. Your child gets caught drinking and smoking. You tell him to stop immediately or there will be consequences. He:

(a) Apologizes and promises not to do it again.

(b) Promises not to do it again, but he points out that most of his friends are doing it so it's not a big deal. He thinks you're making too much of it.

(c) Laughs and says it is "cool to smoke and drink."

(d) Uses bad language, making it quite clear that there is nothing you can do about it—he has every intention of continuing both.

12. During a parent/teacher meeting, the teacher reports on the behavior of several students, in response to a request to perform clean-up activities after a special event. You ask if your child helped. Armed with the answer, you ask your child if he helped. He:

(a) Tells you he helped clean-up after the event.

(b) Tells you he did a lot more to help than other kids and it wasn't fair.

(c) Admits he argued with the teacher about the cleaning because he did not want to do it.

(d) Simply refused to do it and was sent to the principal's office to be reprimanded.

13. Your child suddenly shows up with a different bike. You ask him where he got it. He says:

(a) "I saved my allowance to buy it."

(b) "I exchanged it for my Walkman radio."

(c) "My friend loaned it to me."

(d) "Why do you want to know?" He then becomes argumentative and evasive and doesn't give you a direct answer.

14. Your son and his buddy are playing soccer outside your home and the ball breaks a neighbor's window. The neighbor asks the boys who broke the window. Your son will say:
    (a) "It was an accident. We both broke the window and will do work for you to cover the cost of fixing it."
    (b) "We will take the money from our allowance to pay for the window."
    (c) "My friend broke the window."
    (d) "It was an accident and it's just too bad—I'm not paying for it!"

15. Your child is diagnosed with ADD (Attention Deficit Disorder) and seems to have difficulty in school. The teacher suggests the consultation with a professional indicates:
    (a) In spite of his ADD, he is still doing well in school and simply has to try harder.
    (b) He needs to have a special tutor help him with minor dyslexia (reading difficulties).
    (c) He is unable to attend to any task for more than five minutes, yet he can attend well when his father is fixing the car.
    (d) He is very good at sports, able to attend for twenty minute periods to the coach's instruction in basketball or soccer— (this indicates that if he attends to a task that he likes, he can do it for more than five minutes). School is simply not exciting enough!

16. Your child has just returned from a neighborhood fight. You ask him what happened and he says:
    (a) "I'm sorry about the fight—I probably should apologize to my friend."
    (b) "I'm sorry about the fight but it was self-defense."
    (c) "It's not my fault—he started it."
    (d) "He deserved the beating."

17. Your child does not seem to have any homework. When asked, he says:

(a) He's going to bring his homework from school.
(b) He's having difficulty and will ask for help at school.
(c) The teacher seldom gives him homework.
(d) The teacher gives them stupid projects and they aren't worth doing.

18. Your child's homework habits are:
    (a) He does homework on a regular basis at home.
    (b) He does homework but not regularly.
    (c) He seldom brings books home, let alone mentions homework.
    (d) He never does homework at home.

19. Your child spends hardly any time at home. You suspect he is spending a lot of time with a girlfriend. You check and find out that he is with her. If you ask him directly about it he will say:
    (a) He goes to his girlfriend's home and they frequently do homework together.
    (b) He plays sports with his friends.
    (c) He just hangs around with friends.
    (d) He is involved with recreational activities at the local "Y".

20. Your child comes from a friend's house looking a little green and smelling of cigarettes. You telephone the friend's parents and learn that their child looks the same way. You both conclude the children found some cigarettes and smoked them! You ask your child what happened and he says:
    (a) "We tried smoking some cigarettes but they tasted awful."
    (b) "We smoked a little, but everyone smokes in that house."
    (c) "We took a drag on a cigarette but it's no big deal."
    (d) "We didn't do anything, I just feel a little sick. Why are you bugging me anyway?"

21. Your child comes home with a new sport jacket. You ask him where he got it and he:
    (a) Admits that he stole it and offers to pay for it somehow.

(b) Reluctantly admits he stole it, but says it wasn't very much money and he can pay for it from his allowance.

(c) Says that a friend gave it to him.

(d) Denies everything, gets very angry and tells you to mind your own business.

22. Your child is a tough kid and frequently comes home scratched and bruised. You ask him what is happening and he says:

(a) I get into fights and they are usually my fault.

(b) I start the fights but my friend doesn't have to beat me so much.

(c) I get attacked for no reason by a bully on the street.

(d) Several kids at school beat me up for no reason at all. I talk to one boy's girlfriend and he gets jealous.

23. Your child is having some friends sleep over to play video games. Before going to bed, you go to check on them and see a real mess, including a broken lamp. You ask what happened. You child:

(a) Takes full responsibility for the mess and damage and apologizes.

(b) Takes responsibility for the mess but not for the broken lamp.

(c) Refuses to take responsibility saying the broken lamp was an accident and argues the place is not a mess, just lived in.

(d) Blames everything on his friends.

24. You tell your child that he is responsible for the upset and hurt you feel because he steals and is violent in school. He:

(a) Promises to try not to fight and says he'll never steal again.

(b) Tries to minimize your feelings.

(c) Makes all kinds of excuses for his behavior.

(d) Denies any connection between the trouble he is in and the hurt you feel.

25. Your child is very mean to her best friend, making her cry. When you ask about it she:

(a) Admits she really feels bad, promises not to do it again and promises to apologize to her friend.
(b) Offers to apologize to her friend.
(c) Blames her friend for being so stupid.
(d) Laughs at her friend's reaction saying it's not a big deal (she takes pride that she's so strong and her friend is so weak).

SCORING:

Count the number of A, B, C, and D answers. Give yourself zero points for each A answer, 2 points for each B answer, 3 points for each C answer, and 4 points for each D answer.

If your child scores from 75-100, you have trouble on your hands! If he scores 50-74, there are some difficulties that can be overcome with proper teaching. If he scores 25-49, I would not be too concerned—he is just a normal child. 0-24, you have an angel!

Bibliography

Chandler, M.J. "Egocentricism and Antisocial Behavior: The Assessment and Training of Social Perspective-Talking Skills." *Developmental Psychology* 9 (1973): 326-332.

Clarke, A.M. and A.D. Clarke. *Early Experiences: Myth and Evidence.* London: Open Books, 1976.

Cleckley, Hervey. *The Mask of Sanity.* Augusta, GA: E.S. Cleckley, 1982.

Colby, A. et al. "A Longitudinal Study of Moral Development." *Monograph of Society for Research and Child Development* 48 (1983): 1-2.

Cromer, G. "Repentant Delinquents: A Religious Approach to Rehabilitation." *Jewish Journal of Sociology* 23, No. 2 (1981).

Czudner, Gad. "Changing the Criminal." *Federal Probation* (September 1985): 64-66.

Czudner, Gad and Ruth Mueller. "The Role of Guilt and Its Implication in the Treatment of Criminals." *International Journal of Offender Therapy and Comparative Criminology* 31 (1987): 71-78.

Eisenberg, Nancy and Janet Strayer, eds. *Empathy and Its Development.* New York: Cambridge University Press, 1990.

English, Horace and A. English. *A Comprehensive Dictionary of Psychological and Psychoanalytical Terms.* New York: David McKay Company, 1958.

Frankl, Viktor E. *Psychotherapy and Existentialism: Selected Papers on Logotherapy.* New York: Washington Square, 1967.

Frankl, Viktor E. *Man's Search for Meaning.* New York: Simon and Schuster, 1984.

Fromm, Erich. *The Art of Loving.* New York: Harper and Row, 1956.

Gilligan, Carol. *In a Different Voice.* Cambridge: Harvard University Press, 1982.

Glasser, William. *Reality Therapy.* New York: Harper and Row, 1965.

Golding, William. *Lord of the Flies.* New York: Berkley Publishing, 1959.

Goleman, Daniel. *Emotional Intelligence.* New York: Bantam Books, 1995.

Gupta, Prem and Ruth Mueller. "The Correction of Criminal Thinking and Behavior Through the Cognitive Moral Approach." *Correctional Options* 4 (1984): 27-29.

Hammer, M. and N. Ross. "Psychological Needs of Imprisoned Adult Females with High and Low Conscience Development." *Corrective and Social Psychiatry and Journal of Behavioral Technology Methods and Theory* 23, No. 3 (1977): 73-78.

Hann, N. "Two Moralities in Action Contexts: Relationships to Thought, Ego Regulation and Development." *Journal of Personality and Social Psychology* 36 (1978): 286-305.

Hare, Robert D. *Without Conscience.* New York: Pocket Books, 1993.

Hoffman, Martin. "Altruistic Behavior and Parent Child Relationships." *Journal of Personality and Social Psychology* 31 (1975): 937-943.

Hoffman, Martin. "Affect and Moral Development." *New Directions for Child Development.* Edited by Dante Cicchetti. San Francisco: Jossey-Bass, 1982.

Hoffman, M.L. "Empathy, Its Development and Prosocial Implications." *Nebraska Symposium on Motivation.* Edited by Charles B. Keasey. Lincoln, NE: Univ. of Nebraska Press, 1977.

Hollitscher, W. *Psychoanalysis and Civilization: An Introduction to Sigmund Freud.* New York: Grove Press, 1963.

Kaplan, John. "A Legal Look at Prosocial Behavior: What Can Happen If One Tries to Help or Fails to Help Another." *Altruism, Sympathy and Helping Psychological and Social Principles.* Edited by Lauren Wiste. New York: Academic Press, 1978.

Kohn, Alfie. *The Brighter Side of Human Nature.* New York: Basic Books, 1992.

Kohlberg, Lawrence. "Stage and Sequence: The Cognitive Developmental Approach to Socialization." *Handbook of Socialization Theory and Research.* Edited by David A. Goslin. Chicago: Rand McNally, 1969.

Langon, P.A. and L.A. Greenfield. *Career Patterns of Crime.* Washington, D.C.: Bureau of Justice Statistics (1983).

Luks, Allan and Peggy Payne. *The Healing Power of Doing Good.* New York: Ballantine Books, 1991.

McKenzie, J. *Guilt, Its Meaning and Significance.* London: Unwin, 1962.

Menninger, K. *Whatever Became of Sin?* New York: Bantam Books, 1984.

Morrish, G. Ronald. *Secrets of Discipline.* Toronto: Hushion House, 1998.

Mowrer, O. Hobart. "Communication, Conscience, and the Unconscious." *Journal of Communication Disorders* 1 (1967): 109-135.

Mowrer, O. Hobart. "New Evidence Concerning the Nature of Psychopathology." *Studies in Psychotherapy and Behavior Change.* Edited by M. Feldman. Buffalo, NY: University of Buffalo Press, 1968.

Piaget, Jean. *The Moral Judgment of The Child.* New York: The Free Press, 1965.

Piaget, Jean. *The Construction of Reality in the Child.* New York: Basic Books, 1954.

Regan, J. "Guilt, Perceived Injustice, and Altruistic Behavior." *Journal of Personality and Social Psychology* 18, No. 1 (1971): 124-132.

Reinharz, Peter. *Killer Kids, Bad Law: Tales of the Juvenile Court System.* New York: Barricade Books, 1996.

Rubenstein, R. *Morality and Eros*. New York: McGraw-Hill, 1970.

Samenow, Stanton E. *Inside the Criminal Mind*. New York: Times Books, 1984.

Samenow, Stanton E. *Before It's Too Late*. New York: Times Books, 1989.

Schulman, Michael and Eva Mekler. *Bringing Up a Moral Child*. Reading, MA: Addison-Wesley Publishing Company, Inc., 1985.

Smith, Peter K., Helen Cowie and Mark Blades. *Understanding Children: Development*. Third Ed., Cambridge, MA: Blackwell Publishers, 1996.

Smith, Randall, W.R. Smith and Elliot Noma. "Delinquent Career Lines: A Correctional Link between Theory and Juvenile Offences." *Sociological Quarterly* 25 (1986): 155-179.

Snyder, C.R., Raymond L. Higgins and Rita J. Stucky. *Excuses: Masquerades in Search of Grace*. New York: John Wiley and Sons, 1983.

Stotland, Ezra and Kenneth E. Mathews. *Empathy, Fantasy and Helping*. Thousand Oaks, CA: Sage, 1978.

Thornton, D. and R.L. Reid. "Moral Reasoning and Type of Criminal Offence." *British Journal of Social Psychology* 21 (1982): 231-238.

Wallach, Michael and Lise Wallach. *Psychology: Sanction for Selfishness*. New York: W.H. Freeman and Company, 1983.

Walters, Glenn D. *The Criminal Life Style*. Thousand Oaks, CA: Sage, 1990.

Webster's New World College Dictionary. Vol. 1, s.v. "discipline," "guilt."

Wilson, Colin. *A Criminal History of Mankind*. New York: Carroll &Graf, 1990.

Woocher, J. "From Guilt-Feelings to Reconciliation: Images of Modern Man." *Review of Existential Psychology and Psychiatry* 15 (1977): 186-209.

Yochelson, Samuel and Stanton E. Samenow. *The Criminal Personality, Volume 1: A Profile for Change*. Northvale, NJ: Jason Aronson, 1976.

Yochelson, Samuel and Stanton E. Samenow. *The Criminal Personality, Volume 2: The Change Process*. Northvale, NJ: Jason Aronson, 1994.